GOD'S EAGLES

*Thoughts on the Destiny of God's Eagle
Saints Through All the Ages*

GOD'S EAGLES

Thoughts on the Destiny of God's Eagle
Saints Through All the Ages

G. D. WATSON

Kingsley Press

Shoals, Indiana

God's Eagles

Published by Kingsley Press
PO Box 973
Shoals, IN 47581
USA

Tel. (800) 971-7985
www.kingsleypress.com
E-mail: sales@kingsleypress.com

ISBN: 978-1-937428-68-6 (paperback)
ISBN: 978-1-937428-69-3 (eBook)

First Kingsley Press edition 2017

Contents

Preface

WHEN Brother Watson was corresponding with us relative to this volume, he wrote somewhat as follows:

"This book, *God's Eagles,* is of a kind that no one else that I know of has ever published. It is a series of Bible expositions describing the destiny of the saints clear through all the ages, from the time of the new birth, on through life and death, translation and resurrection, the judgment of the saints, the marriage supper of the Lamb, the chaining of Satan, the millennial reign, and the New Jerusalem, so as to present to the Lord's people a continuous history of the saints clear through. I do not know of any other book in the world that presents such a delineation of the destiny of God's people. I have had the book in mind for twelve years, and at last it is ready for print. I believe it will have a large sale."

We therefore send forth *God's Eagles,* praying that its circulation may prove a mighty inspiration to the children of God anywhere, and that the author may have every reason to praise God both now and hereafter, that he was permitted to pen the messages which are thus given publication.

—The Publishers

Chapter 1

God's Eagles

THERE are many places in the Bible where God mentions eagles, and in such a way as to indicate that the term applies to a class of the servants of God, who have in them those qualities that correspond with eagles in the rank of nature. God has put a language into all things of his creation. There is a spoken language for angels and men, and then there is an unwritten language in all the works of God, just as distinctly and clearly as the spoken language. God puts a language into trees and rocks, loaves and birds, and beasts, and fishes, and the sea and the sky, a language known to himself, and doubtless a language in due time to be perfectly interpreted to the saints of God.

God calls His people by the names of cattle, and sheep, and doves, and eagles. Just as there are sheep among human saints which are not four-legged animals, so there are eagles in human character, which are distinct from rapacious birds. God compares himself to a great eagle, and compares his true saints to eagles. The Lord says in Exodus, "I bare you on eagles' wings and brought you to myself." In David's lament over the death of Saul and Jonathan, he said, "They were swifter than eagles, and stronger than lions." The Psalmist says that those who wait upon the Lord shall renew their strength and mount up with wings as eagles. Jesus tells us in the Gospel that at his coming when his crucified and glorified body shall appear in the sky, "the eagles will be gathered unto it," referring to the rapture of the saints.

We are told in Revelation that of the four living creatures, which represent the highest rank of saved men, one of those living creatures has the form of "a flying eagle." And in the eighth chapter of Revelation where our English reads that John heard an angel flying in the midst of heaven, the Greek word is eagle: "He heard one eagle flying through heaven which was the voice of a glorified man, taking part with Christ in judging the world in the great tribulation.

In every one of these Scripture references, the eagle is used in a good sense to signify the saints of God, who are taking rank in the kingdom of God, corresponding to the rank of eagles in the realm of nature.

The most striking passage bearing on this subject is found in Deuteronomy 32:11-12, "As an eagle that stirreth up her nest, fluttereth over her young, spreadeth abroad her wings, taketh them, beareth them on her wings; so Jehovah alone did lead him, and there was no strange God with him." These words give us a beautiful insight into God's method of dealing with his people, as to how he draws them to himself, and as to how he makes the eagles, and what attributes they are possessed with.

There are various ranks among the servants of God, corresponding to the different ranks among birds, or among trees, or among the stars, and Paul tells us that as one star differs from another star in glory, so will it be in the resurrection of the saints.

1. Now, in the first place, let us notice how God makes his eagles. God makes all things by a plan in his own mind, as he told Moses to make the tabernacle according to the pattern shown him in the mount. When God makes a tree, or a world, or a race of beings, he works according to some plan, and hence when he makes a class of saints which rank as eagles, he works by a method which is set forth in the text.

The first step in the process of making an eagle saint is to stir up the nest. The eagle builds its nest on a lofty mountain crag, or in the highest tree it can find, and forms it of sticks and branches of trees and then lines it with softer things like wool, or paper, or rags, or the skins of animals, making it soft for its young. When the young eagles have become large enough to fly, the mother bird forces them out of the soft nest by tearing away the soft lining and throwing everything out of the nest that would make it comfortable, and letting the young birds down on the sharp sticks and thorns, so that they become dissatisfied with their home and are willing to move somewhere else. This is the way God deals with those of his servants that he calls into close and heroic union with himself. He begins by stirring up their nests, and making them unhappy, that they become willing to move out into a new place of experience, and thought, and life. This is the way he stirred the nests of the Israelites in the land of Egypt. When the Hebrews first went into Egypt, God built a fine nest for them under the administration of Joseph, for they had the fat of the land, and for many years they had prosperity and a good time. But when the time came for God to take them out of Egypt, he knew they would not be willing to leave unless their nest was stirred, and the soft lining was all removed. Hence, God allowed the Egyptians to treat them awfully, with hard bondage and poverty, and distress, and this bondage waxed worse and worse, until in their desperate sorrow, they cried as the voice of one man to the God of Abraham for deliverance. This is the way God stirs the nest of those of his servants that he wants to lift into the altitudes of faith and service. It may be he breaks up the home life, or the church life, or takes away property, or removes loved ones, or by a series of strange providences takes away the soft lining of their lives, their earthly, or social, or religious comforts, and lets them down upon the sharp thorns, and the hard sticks of trouble and suffering, until like the Hebrews in Egypt, they cry out to the living God for deliverance.

All the apostles had their nests stirred, all the reformers and great evangelists and great religious leaders had their nests stirred, until they were willing to emigrate into new quarters, or go to the ends of the earth, or change their locality, or change their religious relationships, or change a traditional theology, or move out into a new realm of thought, or prayer, or work, or experience. We can never move into any new locality without breaking our relationship with the present locality. We can never go into a better climate without disrupting from the climate we are now in. We can never move toward God without leaving something of Adam. We can never migrate toward the west without leaving the east. We can never step toward holiness without breaking with unholiness.

God takes away the soft things on which we lean, the dear old props of nature, of friends, of old forms, and old ceremonies, and old comforts. He undermines our natural foundations, and lets us down on the bare rock. If God did not thus stir our nest, we would be unwilling to move out into his realm. Abraham is a pattern, and he was God's immigrant, and all true saints are immigrants from the old nest of natural things into the upper air of the things of God.

The second step in the making of an eagle is, the mother bird *flutters over them*. The young birds hear the sound of wings to draw their attention from the thorns and sticks to her. The mother eagle will watch her young, and when they begin to whine and complain, and move uneasily, and hunt for some easy place, and cannot find it, then the mother bird rises over the nest and flutters her feathers, and shakes out her wings right over their heads, with a most peculiar sound, to draw the attention of their eyes from the painful thorns and sticks in the bottom of the nest. Oh, what a language there is in the sound of wings, a language perfectly intelligible to the young eagles. When they hear that peculiar sound, the young birds look up to the parent. This is just what God does in the making of his saints. When God allows trouble, sorrow, sickness, poverty, bereavement and desolation to come to us, and we weep and cry and murmur, and find fault, and get sad, and blue, and look around us to find something to lean upon, and hunt for comfort in the creature, in that which is of the earth, and find nothing but sharp briars and piercing trials, then God flutters over us, and we hear the sound of his wings. God does it to draw our attention to himself, and for us to look away to him, to look away above us, from the coffin, from the grave, from the old house, from the deserted farm, from departed friends, from earthly property, from a good reputation, from human comfort. We look up to catch the sound of those mysterious wings that flutter in the ears of our souls. God draws us to look up to him with sounds we have not heard before, and like the prophet Ezekiel, God causes us to hear the noise of wings.

The next step in the process of making eagle saints is, *he spreadeth abroad his wings.* No bird in all the world has wings like the eagle, and the mother eagle is always larger than the male bird, and her wings are the largest. Many an eagle measures fourteen feet from tip to tip when its wings are spread out. When you see the wings folded, you would not think they were over two feet long, but when those wings are stretched out it is amazing how long they seem. If the young eagles could talk they might say to their mother, "I never saw you look so big before, for when you were here with us in the nest, you looked rather small, but since those wings are spread out at their full length, we are amazed at the magnitude of your protection and strength." The spreading abroad of the eagle's wings is a revelation to her young of her strength. This is the way God deals with us. He not only flutters over us to draw our attention to himself, but "he spreadeth abroad his wings." When we get our attention on God he unfolds his magnitude to our faith, he spreads abroad the great wings of his attributes, his majesty, his power, his glory.

There have been times in some of our lives in which we lost apparently everything on the earth, when property and friends, and health, and prospects were swept away as in a storm, and at those times we heard the flutter of the divine wings, and looked up and saw God spread abroad his wings, and unfold to our earnest faith the marvelous strength of his perfections. It is an epoch in our lives when God unfolds himself to us, when he gives us a vision of his infinite providence, the vastness of his resources, the revelation of his inward feelings, the largeness of his arrangements, the delicacy and minuteness of his care over us, the far sweep of his eternal purposes.

What a thrill of inspiration goes through our souls when we see the great wings of the Jehovah Eagle spread abroad above our heads, those wings that stretch from horizon to horizon, that spread out without beginning and without ending, from the eternal past into the eternal future, those wings that can support worlds on worlds as easily as carrying an insect, and those wings whose feathers are the attributes of Almighty God, are stretched out for our safety, our salvation, our security.

We never see the infinite merit of Jesus until revealed to us by the Holy Ghost in the outspreading wings of the atonement of the precious blood. Just as the spreading abroad of the eagle's wings is the great revelation that the young eagles have of the parent bird, so the spreading abroad of God's eagle wings constitutes that revelation of himself to us of his unlimited perfections. It is then that the wings of the mother bird become larger and softer than all the comforts found in the nest. It is when God spreads abroad his wings over us, and around us, that we see he is infinitely greater than everything in nature, or than everything in our dreams, or our air castles, that he has sufficiency in himself, infinitely beyond all our wants and all our imaginations.

Are you an orphan? Is your husband dead, or your wife dead? Are your parents dead? Are you poor, or hated, or cast out? Are you criticized, or ostracized, or minimized, or undersized? Are you perplexed? Are you barefooted, hungry, homeless, a beggar on the street, or are you on your way to the poor house? If you are in such a condition, and you could see God spread abroad his wings, and unfurl the blue sky of his attributes above you, and around you, you would cease to feel sorrow, you would be lifted above your circumstances, you would have an inspiration from above that would be more than a match for all the ills of this world. The sight of God's infinite wings spread abroad would make us forget the tearing up of any earthly nest.

The next step in the process of making eagles is, *the mother bird taketh them, and beareth them on her wings.* She stands on the edge of the nest, and lays her wings down so the young eagles can climb up on her wings and fasten their young claws into her feathers, preparatory for a great flight up in the air.

See how God stirred the nest of the early Christian church in Jerusalem by the beheading of James, and the persecution, and how the infant church was apparently torn to pieces, and how they were scattered everywhere, preaching the Word. But for the stirring of their Jerusalem nest, they would not likely have gone fifty miles away, but by stirring the nest up they were scattered to the four corners of the earth. The mother bird spreads out her long wings flat down on the nest, and the young eagles are glad to step from the briers and thorns, and sharp sticks, upon their mother's soft great wings. When the young birds have fastened their claws on the mother's wings, then she prepares for a great flight. Taking the young birds one at a time on her wing, the mother bird will soar from four thousand to five thousand feet up in the blue sky, and then give a sudden lurch, and throw off the young eagle. The young bird tumbles and rolls over, and puts out its wings, and beats the air while it is falling, but the mother bird watches her young, and when the helpless little thing is half way down to the earth, she shoots downward with the accuracy and the speed of a bullet, and catches the young bird again on her wing, and again soars aloft in the sky, and repeats this process till the young eagle has learned how to fly. This illustrates in the spiritual life the way God teaches the perfect believer to live by faith, and to exercise the Spirit's gifts and graces, and to form habits of perfect trust against what seems to be utter ruin and absolute failure. When the eagle has formed habits of flying, it will stem terrific storms, and beat its way up against the channel of the wind, and surmount the elements against all ordinary calculations. It is thus that God takes the eagle saints on his wings, and carries them aloft in glorious flights of rich and rare experience, and then suddenly seems to drop them and leave them to themselves, that they may learn the divine art of perfect trust against all odds and difficulties and all failures.

It is then that the believer learns to trust in God alone, without leaning on past experiences, or any feeling, or religious emotion, without leaning on saints, or on the church, or on circumstances, but to run the tremendous risk of falling helpless into hands of infinite love. It is then that God turns loose his eagles in a thunder storm, at midnight, or a cold, winter's day, with a wind blowing a gale, or to face a blizzard of circumstances, and to practice that venturesome and seemingly reckless reliance on God's Word, and on his character. This is the way that God makes those eagle saints which are to take rank in his coming kingdom.

We now come to consider what are the qualities of eagles. There are certain moral and spiritual qualities that constitute a fitness for rank in the kingdom of God, and as there are various ranks in the kingdom of heaven, and each of these ranks is marked by certain qualities peculiar to its own, so there are certain qualities in the eagle which are typical of the front rank saints. In the first place, the eagle is the king of the air, just as the lion is the king among beasts. Jesus appropriates the name of lion to himself in referring to his conquest of the earth, and we see in the writings of Moses that Jehovah appropriates the name of eagle to himself, in referring to his supernatural power, in working the great miracles in Egypt, and lifting his people out of bondage to bear them on his wings into the land of Canaan.

The lion is not the largest of animals, but it is the king among all animals just the same. There are some birds which are larger than the eagle, but the eagle is emphatically the king of the air, and over all other birds. There is a royalty and majesty in the eagle which belongs to no other bird or fowl. This is true of the eagle saints, for they constitute a race of rulers that are to reign in the coming kingdom.

The man that governs the air governs the world. At first, men fought with clubs and stones; later on, they fought with arrows and spears; still later on, they fought with gunpowder and bullets; then came the era of warfare in battle ships, and the conquest of navies on the sea, but in these times they are carrying on the art of war up in the air and down under the sea, which is a clear sign of the winding up of this age and the concluding of the drama of man's rule in the earth and the preparation for the final scene of this world's history in its present fallen condition.

Satan, according to Scripture, is the prince of the powers of the air, and, from the fall of man, he has had his throne in the aerial regions above this earth.

The word heaven in the Bible has several meanings to it. When the word heaven is used in referring to where God has his throne, the word in the original is always in the plural number as, for instance, "Our Father who art in the heavens," is the literal rendering, but where the word heaven applies to the aerial regions, the blue sky, or the elements of the atmosphere around this earth, the word is in the singular, prefixed with the definite article "the," as "the heaven." It is this local heaven that belongs to our earth that Satan has for his playground and the place of his authority, and where he marshals his fallen angels to carry on the wickedness of this world. And because Satan has his seat up in the sky, he also has power over the earth, and is the god of this present age and of the fallen state of this world.

During the tribulation judgment, the archangel Michael will drive Satan from his place up in the air, as described in Revelation twelfth chapter, and he will be compelled to walk on the earth in humiliation; and then these heavens are to be cleansed, according to Paul's teaching, and the glorified saints are to be elevated to take charge of the things up in the air, and to govern this world in the coming age. And thus, as the eagles are now the kings of the air, and have a dominion greater than all other birds, so, in the coming age, the eagle saints are to be lifted to possessions of authority and dominion with Christ in ruling this world, and superintending all the affairs of the nations that survive the tribulation judgment and live in the millennial age.

The Scriptures abound in promises concerning the rulership of the true saints in the ages to come.

After Christ arose from the dead, he spent forty days upon the earth, but during that time he lived almost entirely up in the air and out of sight of human beings. With his glorified body, he appeared to chosen witnesses, at various times and places, during the forty days, taking his body through stone walls without opening a door, and transporting that body from place to place at will, and instantaneously showing that he was as much at home up in the air as down on the earth.

The earthly example of Christ during those forty days is a perfect picture of the way the glorified saints will exist in the coming millennial age, for being glorified they will have bodies like Christ and transport themselves at will through any part of heaven or earth, like Jesus did, and be perfectly superior to what we call the law of nature.

Those people who are not killed in the great tribulation judgment, and who submit to Christ, and who live on through the millennium, and at that time multiply and fill the earth, will form the nations which will be superintended by these glorified saints. As we suffer with him, we shall also reign with him. "Ye who have followed me in my temptations, I will give you a kingdom, and you shall sit on thrones, judging the tribes of Israel." "He that overcometh, to him will I give authority over the nations, and he shall shepherdize them with a rod of iron." These Scriptures will all be fulfilled perfectly in the coming age when the glorified saints shall be the eagles in the upper air of that dispensation.

In the next place, the eagles *are great watchers*. There is not an eye in all the world like the eagle's eye. The eagle has an eye both telescopic to discern things afar off and microscopic to see the smallest. The eye of the eagle can penetrate a great distance and discover things that no other eye on earth could find at such a long range. It is said by the best of authority that it is impossible to deceive an eagle. They may be captured when young, or shot, or conquered in battle, but they cannot be deceived in a matter of vision. Audubon knew more about birds than any man in the world, and he gives it out that he never could succeed in deceiving the eagle.

He once climbed a mountain crag near an eagle's nest and hid himself, as he thought, perfectly private to the habits of the mother bird. When the mother eagle returned, she soared aloft, round and round above her nest, piercing every nook and corner of the mountain, until she spied Audubon in his hiding place, and then dropping the prey that she was bringing to her young, gave a loud scream to her mate which was miles away, notifying him that their nest had been discovered. This quality of eagle vision is referred to by our Savior concerning those saints which he pronounces to be the *elect*. Remember that the word *elect* in the Bible does not refer to salvation, but it refers to a rank which people take after they are justified, and mostly the term refers to sanctification, and to being in the company of the bridehood saints.

Jesus says that there shall arise many false Christs and false prophets, and shall deceive many; that is, deceive many Christians, and if it were possible, they would deceive the very elect, but it is impossible for the true elect saints to be deceived in matters of religious faith. Thousands in every generation have been deceived by foolish and heretical religious leaders, but no one has ever been so deceived who was perfectly sanctified and had the real genuine baptism of the Holy Spirit. John Dowie and Sanford, and Charles Russell and others have deceived thousands of Christians, to more or less extent, but not one soul who was thoroughly sanctified, and delivered from the old man, and had the one abiding baptism of the Holy Spirit has ever been deceived by such men.

Not one of God's eagles will ever be deluded by Mormonism, or Christian Science, or Spiritualism, or Dowieism and Russellism, or any other "Ism," because they are divinely illuminated with that apostolic light which Jesus and the prophets and the apostles had.

The apostle Peter refers to some Christians who are near-sighted, and cannot see afar off, but he distinctly affirms that such Christians are near-sighted because they have not escaped the corruption or the depravity which is in the world, and because they have not added to their faith, virtue, knowledge, temperance, patience, godliness, and brotherly kindness.

He describes a soul that is thoroughly sanctified, and filled with the Holy Spirit, and then says, he that lacketh these things is near-sighted, and cannot see afar off; in other words, he may be a Christian, a weak Christian; he may get to heaven, but he is not one of God's eagles, and does not possess that keen, penetrating vision which can see things afar off, and distinguish between truth and error.

It is amazing how multitudes of good people can be hood-winked and fooled in so many ways, and by so many people. It is said that the patriarchs had such vision that they saw the promises of God afar off. They had an eagle vision to see things thousands of years ahead of them, not only as to the first coming of Christ, but also to his second coming, and to that city which had foundations, and whose builder and maker is God.

Another quality of eagles is, they prefer great heights. They build their nests on high mountain peaks and in the highest trees they can find.

They love to soar miles and miles above the earth, in the vast upper blue sky, far above the flight of all other birds. Their instincts are lofty, they spurn low spots for their resting places. This is a trait of eagle saints. Their song is,

> You need not look for me down in Egypt's sand,
> For I have pitched my tent far up in Beulah Land.
>
> Lord, lift me up and let me stand,
> By faith on heaven's table land.

An eagle saint is one that has been delivered from the old Adam, and filled with Divine love – the love that came down from the Godhead, and the love that instinctively arises to dwell with God in the heavenly places.

The first man had two names. His first name was Adam, which signifies "red earth," and indicates the earth nature of fall-en man. His second name was Ish, translated by the word "man," but this name Ish indicates the higher spiritual part of a man's life. The Greek word which we translate "sanctification" signifies *to take earth out;* the word is *hage,* a combination of two words. The word *ge,* always in the Greek Testament means *earth,* and the prefix *ha* is the strongest negative, and means *no earth.* Now that is the word that the Holy Ghost has selected for holiness, or sanctification. Thus you see the word "Adam" means "red earth," and the word *hage,* or "holiness" means "no earth." Thus when a believer is truly sanctified, and the earth or the old Adam is taken out of him, and he is filled with the Holy Spirit, he is lifted into the heavenly places, and his faith and prayer and spiritual life ascends to those spiritual regions which corresponds with the lofty flight of the eagle.

Eagle saints have high motives, and lofty prayers, and heavenly aspirations. In giving their money, and in their spiritual work, they are wider than sectarian bonds, and higher than sectarian walls, and far above selfish motives.

There is a word in the Song of Solomon which says, "Let us look from the top." This is the lofty eagle vision of those who have, in the truest and best sense, entered the higher life. Such believers soar in their faith and prayer and love above narrow boundaries, above national lines, and see the great world, with its teeming millions, from God's standpoint, and see the affairs of this world in the light of heaven and eternity. In the language of Isaiah, they dwell on high, and their defense is the munitions of rocks. They mount up with wings as eagles, and grasp things that are above the world.

In the fourth place, *eagles are strong of wing.* An eagle can knock a man down with his wing. The power of the ostrich is in his foot, and they have been known to kill horses with a kick. The power of the lion is in his mouth, by which be can tear flesh. But the power of an eagle is mainly in his wing. A man in the Alps stood on a mountain and watched an eagle fighting two rams, and saw how the eagle would strike the great sheep with his wings and hurl them over on the ground. The strength of the eagle's wing is seen in his flight, in the great speed, and in the length of them.

This power of the eagle's wing sets forth the supernatural strength of the eagle saints in prayer, and faith, and endurance, and long suffering. There is a strange divine power in saintly souls which outmatches all physical strength, or all intellectual sharpness, or all subtlety of philosophy, or all the ordinary strength of human beings. There are little women, and sickly men, and poor people, who have reached a place in God where in spiritual things they are giants, and are like lions and eagles in the natural world. There are those who seem to be full of weakness, and yet by the power of prayer and the loftiness of faith they are carrying burdens, bearing troubles, enduring sorrows and accomplishing things through the Holy Ghost beyond all the natural strength of man, and beyond all the intellectual greatness of scholars and orators and this world's great ones. They have that strength of the eagle's wing by which in union with Jesus Christ through the baptism of the Spirit they bear all things, and endure all things, and hope all things. This is a divine strength just beyond all fanaticism, or fleshy demonstrations; it is above all boasting, or all self-conceit; it is higher than air castles, stronger than a mere notion, but firm with a rock bottom, and a sky-blue clearness which is attained only through the indwelling of the Holy Spirit. These qualities of God's eagles are obtained by that perfect attitude of abandonment and obedience and faith that waits on the Lord, until the strength is renewed, and in that strength the soul mounts up with wings as eagles and runs and is not weary, and walks and is not faint.

CHAPTER 2

Job's Eagle Vision

FROM the first promise that God gave Adam and Eve, and on through the history of the Old Testament, the patriarchs and prophets looked far ahead for their salvation because they knew that there would be no salvation except through the coming of the Son of God, in human flesh, to make an atonement for the human race. We Christians look back to the crucifixion of Christ as the basis for our saving faith, and we look forward to the coming of the Lord again as the consummation of our faith. But the believers in the Old Testament had nothing to look back to, but everything pertaining to salvation and the resurrection was in the future to them.

The Holy Spirit gave to Job a wonderful vision of the Lord Jesus as a personal Redeemer, and his vision was given to Job in the darkest period of his life. There is in the 19th chapter of Job, a description of the darkest period and the greatest humiliation and sorrow that that patriarch was ever called to endure; and yet in that hour of greatest distress and gloom, there came to him the brightest vision of the future. He says, "For I know that my redeemer liveth, and that he shall stand at the latter day upon the earth, and though after my skin, worms destroy this body, yet in my flesh shall I see God; whom I shall see for myself, and mine eyes shall behold, and not another, though my reins be consumed within me."

It is a singular fact that the people of God get their brightest visions of divine things in the very darkest hours of their lives. Whether it is because of the law of compensation, or whether it is because of some unknown reason in the mind of God, so it is, that out of the greatest humiliation and trouble of soul there comes the clearest insight into divine things. The darkest hour in the life of Moses was when the people of Israel turned back from Kadesh Barnea, and yet it was at that time that God said to Moses, "As true as I live, saith the Lord, the whole earth shall be full of my glory." It was when the apostle John was banished to the lonely Isle of Patmos, away from friends and Christian fellowship, amid the desolation of barren rocks, that God opened up to him the brightest visions of the day of the Lord, and he had fellowship with angels and heavenly beings. It was when John Bunyan was shut in a filthy jail for twelve years in Bedford, England, that the Holy Spirit gave him the charming vision of *Pilgrim's Progress* and of the *Holy War.*

When we walk through a deep, narrow canyon, we can look up in the day time and see the stars shining in the sky because the glare of the sun is shut away. Out of the deepest depths of lonely sorrow and earthly deprivation we have the grandest visions of heavenly things. The deeper we are baptized into crucifixion, the higher we ascend in spiritual discernment and experience.

Job was one of the great eagle saints of ancient times, and his vision is a sample of what God has provided for the true saints in all generations.

There are four items mentioned in this eagle vision of the patriarch.

1. *"I know that my redeemer liveth."* – This refers to the coming of the Son of God in human flesh, as a Redeemer and Savior. The word redeemer in the Old Testament has a peculiar meaning. It refers to a person who has lost his property through poverty, or death, and no one could buy it back and restore the forfeited land except someone of near kin, such as a brother, or uncle, or cousin. This near kinsman who would buy back the forfeited estate and restore it to the original heir was called a "redeemer." This is the sense in which the word redeemer is used all through the Scriptures. The eternal Son of God came forth from the Father, and took upon himself a human body and a human soul ; and thereby made himself a near kinsman to the human race, a brother of mankind, and in his human nature he suffered, the just for the

unjust, and made an atonement sufficient to meet all the claims of divine law against the fallen race of Adam.

In this substitution of the spotless Son of God, and Son of man, Jesus paid the price to the claims of the divine government whereby he could save the human soul from all sin, and raise the dead body, and glorify it in immortality; and also restore the earth from the tyranny of Satan, and remove every curse from man and the earth, and restore all things back to original holiness and glory. All this is involved in Christ being a Redeemer

Job had a vision of the personality of the Son of God before his incarnation, for his words are in the present tense, and he had the divine assurance that the Son of God was a living person in his day, for he says, "I know that my redeemer liveth."

The Son of God had his distinguished personality and character before his incarnation. It was not the human body and soul of Jesus which gave him his personality, but it was his divine personality which took to himself, from the Virgin Mary, a human body and a human soul, so that Christ was alive from eternity, and Jesus said to the Jews, "Before Abraham was, I am."

2. The next item in this eagle vision, refers to the *second coming of the Messiah*, when he should stand at the latter day upon the earth. It is true that Christ stood on the earth in his human body at his first coming to make an atonement for the human race, but that did not take place at the latter day, and hence these words must refer to the second coming of Christ when he will stand on the earth in his glorified humanity as the ruler of the world. The word stand implies something firm, fixed and settled, without any question, in the most perfect authority and power. At the first coming of Christ he was hounded from place to place, and hunted as if to be a prey to the vengeance of mankind. He was a pilgrim in his own world and a stranger among his own people, and he had no special home, as he said, "No place to lay his head," so that we can hardly say that he stood upon the earth, but only walked to and fro in it for a short time until he should take his flight back to the right hand of God.

But by his death, having redeemed the world, not only human beings, but also the earth itself, he will come again to reap the harvest of his redemption and take his place on the earth with absolute firmness and undisputed authority. As a Redeemer, Jesus has made provision to save the soul from all sin, and to save the body from death and the earth from all the curse which sin has brought on it. The perfect consummation of all these things will be when Jesus returns and stands on Mount Olivet to take possession of the earth as its perfect ruler. It is then that the vision will be consummated when John saw the angel put his foot on the land and sea as a typical act of taking possession of the whole earth. A farmer makes two visits to his wheat field. First, he goes out in the spring of the year to plow the soil and sow the seed; and this corresponds with what our Redeemer did at his first coming: and then in the autumn the farmer visits his field again to reap the harvest and thresh out the grain, and throw away the chaff, and gather the wheat into his garner. This corresponds with what the Redeemer will do at his second coming. He will reap the harvest of what he sowed by the shedding of his blood and the giving of his word, and destroy the wicked out of the earth and gather the saints into his everlasting kingdom.

3. The third item in Job's eagle vision of redemption refers to the resurrection of the body.

The patriarch had a clear revelation that his poor body, which was then full of sores, would be resurrected from death and shine forth in immortality, perfectly free from all disease or pain, or the possibility of dying any more. "After my skin worms shall destroy this body, yet in my flesh shall I see God." Here is a recognition that after his body had returned to the dust, the same body would be resurrected in a glorious condition, and that in that glorified body he would look on the face of his divine Redeemer. God revealed to Job the literal resurrection of the dead body. He was not tinctured with that modern infidel notion, which so many preachers in these times have, that the dead body will not rise again, and that nothing will survive death except the human soul.

The spirit of man is never buried, and never turns to dust, and is never consumed by worms; and hence the word *resurrection* is never in the Bible applied to a man's spirit, but only to his dead body. If the dead body does not rise into life again, then there is no such thing as resurrection, for the term is applied only to the body. There were no heresies in ancient times among the professed people of God. Scripture prophesies that heresies belong to the latter days, and the multiplying of these heresies is a proof that we are living in the very latter part of this age, and on the verge of the coming of the Lord.

As Job looked upon his afflicted body, he saw only a mass of putrefying sores from the crown of his head to the soles of his feet. He was such an object of loathsome disgust that he tells us in this chapter, he was stripped of his glory, and the crown had fallen from his head, and that he sat in darkness, and that God's providences were like an army of enemies encamped against him, and that his acquaintances were estranged from him, and that his own servants counted him a stranger, and would not respond to his call, and that his wife would not be entreated by him, and that the little children despised him, and he cried out for someone to have pity upon him, but there was no one in all the world who would respond to his cries. And yet with this picture of unutterable distress in his flesh, God revealed to him a glorious future resurrection, when that poor, diseased and loathsome body would arise from the dust and be radiant with immortal glory and shine forth in youth and honor, and out of that body he would worship the Jehovah Savior and enter into the unspeakable joy of communion with his God and Savior. He not only got the vision of a glorious resurrection, but he also was made to know that the righteous would rise before the wicked, and that he would be in the first resurrection.

In the twenty-seventh chapter, Job speaks of rich men who will die in their sins and be buried, but that they shall not rise at the same time that the righteous do. He says of the rich, "He is buried in death, but he shall not be gathered," that is, gathered with the righteous in the first resurrection (verses 15-19).

Hence the vision of the resurrection given to Job agrees with all Scripture that there are two resurrections – the first for the righteous, and the second for the wicked.

David says in the first Psalm, in describing the character of the blessed man, that the ungodly shall not stand up in the judgment nor sinners in the congregation of the righteous. In this world both the righteous and the wicked are in the same congregation in the churches and all assemblies, but in the judgment period, the blessed man will rise from the dead and leave the ungodly still in death.

Thus we see that away back in the centuries before the Bible was written, God gave to Job a vision of things far in the future concerning redemption and salvation and the resurrection, just as perfect as the teachings we have in the New Testament. This was not something that Job learned by study, but it was revealed to him by the Spirit of the living God, and revelations of Cod are perfect.

4. The next item in Job's great vision was that in his glorified body he should look on the face of his Redeemer and behold him in all his glory. "In my flesh shall I see God, whom I shall see for myself, and my eyes shall behold, and not another." This is what spiritual writers have called the "beatific vision." The word signifies the vision of Cod, or seeing the face of God in his uncreated glory, and beauty, and power. To see the face of God, in the person of the Lord Jesus, is the climax of all vision in the universe.

Nothing in creation can surpass or equal the seeing of the face of God. The face expresses all things in the soul, mind and heart. The most beautiful thing God has ever made in heaven or earth is a beautiful face. The universe is full of beauty, and we never tire of the charms of sea, and sky, and land, and flowers, and mountains, and clouds, and all the beauties which are spread around us in the creation that came out of the mind of God. And God has put all of his mind in the person, and in the face of Jesus Christ, so that every perfection of the Divine Being is revealed in the face of Jesus. The body of the Lord Jesus must of necessity be the most perfect and the most glorious of anything which is formed in all the universe, for he is the crown and glory and ornament of everything which is formed in creation, and there never can be any creature which will surpass the body of the Lord Jesus, and there never can be any glory which will excel the glory of the Son of man. Suppose we could have set before us in one vision every perfection, and every charm, and every beauty in all the created universe; suppose that all the beauty which has ever been seen in human faces, in rolling seas, and blue skies, and sun, moon and stars, and mountain and valley, and flowers and rocks, and rainbows, and flowing rivers – all this collection of beauty put into one single picture, would we ever tire of gazing upon it? And yet all this assemblage of charms would only be as a drop compared to the vast ocean of uncreated beauty and glory there is in the divine nature.

In addition to all these beauties and glories, there is another universe of moral and spiritual beauty, such as the beauty of humility, of charity, of tenderness, of love, the brightness of wisdom, the loftiness of righteousness, the stability of truth, the grandeur of courage and faith, all those beauties of character, which require a spiritual discernment to see and appreciate them. All this universe of spiritual loveliness exists in the divine nature to an infinite degree, and all this moral beauty will be manifested in the face of Jesus Christ.

It is this vision of the glory of God in the face of Jesus that Job referred to when he said, "Mine eye shall behold him for myself, and not another." The word does not mean a mere passing glance, but it signifies a fixed and steady gaze at the glory of God. "I shall not only see him, but I shall behold him." This refers to that abiding vision of the glory of God fixed in the eye of the mind forever. It is that vision desire in our being. This is the consummation of all bliss and happiness possible to a created intelligence.

This is the great ocean of infinite and endless joy, to which all other joys are like little rivulets. It was this eagle vision of Job's which sustained him amid his unspeakable sorrow, and desolation, and suffering. It is this vision which we need to lift us up, and inspire us, amid the trials through which we are now passing on our way to the coming kingdom.

CHAPTER 3

Gideon's Eagle Band

THE battle that Gideon fought with the Midianites was one of the most remarkable in the history of the world. It was not only a miraculous battle, but it was one arranged by a special Divine providence, and every detail of it was made prophetic of the last battle that will ever he fought in this world's history.

The Lord took the initiative with Gideon, calling him from his secret place, where he was threshing out grain, and subjected him to various tests of faith, and answered his request for signs, and arranged all the details of the battle: so that it was in reality not Gideon's battle, but the Lord's battle against his enemies, and for this reason it occupies a place in so many Scriptures, as prophetic of things to come, in the winding up of the history of warfare in this world.

We are rapidly approaching the time when a great many prophecies concerning the winding up of this age will be fulfilled, and if we look forward to the coming of Jesus, and the great tribulation judgment, and the fulfilling of God's plan for Israel, and for the kingdom age, we can get very clear ideas of these things by looking back at the patterns of them which are furnished in the Old Testament history.

We are taught by Isaiah that the ten plagues put on the Egyptians is a pattern of the great tribulation judgment coming on the earth. And we are taught in several passages that Gideon's battle with the Midianites is a pattern of the great and last conflict with the enemies of God in this world. In the seventh chapter of Judges, we see God's method of selecting a band of eagle saints, heroes of the first rank, who were samples and types of that company of heroes which will be with Jesus in the latter day conflict.

There are three points connected with this history: First, the two divisions of the soldiers; second, their armor; third, the battle.

Each of these points is filled with instruction for the saints of God.

1. Let us notice the two divisions of the army. Gideon had under him 32,000 soldiers who had volunteered to go with him into the battle. They were all Israelites, circumcised, and members of what might be called God's visible church on earth. They had all volunteered, and were in good standing, as respectable members of God's Israel. It has been estimated that the Midianites numbered nearly one million, and Gideon's small army was only a drop in the bucket compared to their enemies. And yet God said to Joshua, "The people are too many for me to give the Midianites into their hands, lest Israel vaunt themselves; saying, Mine own hand hath saved me." This was pre-eminently God's battle, and of all the battles in human history, this was one in which God alone should get the glory, and so he determined to weed out all possible glory of the flesh.

Gideon made a proclamation that all who were *afraid* should return and depart from Mt. Gilead, and there returned of the people twenty-two thousand, leaving ten thousand with Gideon. The division was made on the basis of fear; and each man was to sit in judgment on himself, and made an open profession of his cowardice by leaving the battle and returning home. You see God did not pick out the cowards, but he so arranged it that every one should pick himself out as a coward. This is God's method in judgment, for we are told that every man shall give an account of himself unto God. When a man sits in judgment on himself, he has no one to complain of, and he cannot accuse another of misjudging him. God is the only being in the universe who has this method of judgment. That is, men of their own accord confessed that they were not true soldiers, that they did not have in them the courage to destroy the enemies of the Lord.

They had the name of Israelites, but as Paul says, "They were not of Israel," and did not have the heart of Israel in them. This is God's sample picture of the visible church on earth. If we take thirty-two thousand church members as they come, twenty-two thousand of them will confess that they are not born of God, and have never had saving faith in Jesus Christ: and that while they have a name to live and to be members of the body of Christ, yet in heart and in reality they are none of his, and so are utterly unqualified to fight the battle of the Lord.

The second division of the army was of a different nature and on a different basis. God will not only make a division between those members of the church which are born again, and those who are not converted, but he will proceed to make another division between those who are partly carnal and those who are entirely yielded to him; and have in them the spirit of perfect consecration, and perfect love, and heart loyalty. After separating all those who did not have the true heart of an Israelite, the Lord said again unto Gideon, "The people are yet too many; bring them down unto the water, and I will try them there, and it shall be that of whom I say unto thee, This shall go with thee, the same shall go with thee, and of whomsoever I say, This shall not go with thee, the same shall not go." So Gideon brought the people down to the water, and the Lord said, "Everyone that lappeth of the water as a dog lappeth, him shalt thou set by himself: likewise every one that boweth down upon his knees to drink, and the number of them that lapped, putting their hand to their mouth, were three hundred men, but all the rest of the people bowed down upon their knees to drink. And the Lord said, "By the three hundred men that lapped will I save you, and deliver the Midianites into thy hand."

This is a very remarkable passage of Scripture: and unless it had been inspired by the Holy Ghost, nothing like it would ever have occurred to any human mind in all the world. It is a clear revelation of things in the kingdom of God, and in the history of God's people in all history there are special providences, both in the outward life and in the inner experiences, by which the Lord proves and tests every virtue of the soul preparatory to their final destiny. God intended to reduce the size of Gideon's army to the lowest minimum, for the perfecting of their faith, so they would be compelled to give God all the glory.

The best of saints often wonder why they are kept in such reduced circumstances and loaded with so many infirmities, not understanding that this is God's plan to destroy all self-dependence and self-glory, that their faith may be perfectly pure and centered in God alone.

Gideon's three hundred needed to be made perfect as soldiers, and hence it was needful to subject them to a special test that would reveal the qualities of a soldier. It is one thing to be a citizen, and another thing to be a soldier.

The apostle Paul teaches us that when we become justified we are citizens of the household of faith; but after that, it is by the baptism with the Holy Spirit that we put on the whole armor of God and become soldiers to fight the Lord's battles.

The bridehood saints must not only be citizens of the kingdom of heaven, but they must all of them be soldiers and have the qualities of a true soldier.

There are certain actions that naturally flow out from citizenship, and there are other actions that flow out from the character of a soldier, and in this testing of Gideon's army, God was planning to make the men reveal those qualities which would best express the nature of a soldier. It was by a special providence that all the ten thousand should be thirsty at the same time, and that the whole army should all want to drink water at the same time, and thus God would discover by the way they drank water as to who they were that had in them the true character of the vigilant soldier.

It is a universal law that the act always flows from the nature. There is an infallible relation between the noun and the verb of everything in creation. Thus it was God's plan that those who were the best soldiers should manifest that character by the way in which they drank water.

This is exactly what God has been doing with all his true saints in all generations, and he is dealing with his people at the present time on the same plan, that each one may be led to manifest the deepest qualities of faith and character which will decide whether they are prepared to be in that chosen company which forms the bride of the Lamb.

The word *try,* found in the fourth verse, is a very striking expression: It is the regular Hebrew word for *sanctification,* and the same word that is used in Malachi, where the Lord says, "I will *purify* the sons of Levi." The real meaning of the passage is, when you bring them down to drink water, I will find who the sanctified ones are, I will put them to a test of their fitness for front rank service, by the way they drink water. Here we see again that God did not pick out those who were the bravest, and those who were really fitted to be eagle saints, or to be in the bridehood company, but he arranged for each man to reveal his own character, and his own fitness for front rank in the kingdom of God. in an unconscious way, which is always the best way to get the revelation of true character. God is an infinite gentleman, and never behaves himself in a rude or uncultured way with his people. If God had in some visible manner picked out those three hundred eagle saints, it would have wounded the feelings of the other nine thousand and seven hundred, and at the same time it might have been a temptation to the three hundred to spiritual pride, but God's ways are absolutely perfect, far beyond the conception of human minds.

God allows each man, in an unwitting way, to manifest the true inwardness of his own being, so that the absolute truth is manifested, and in such a way that no one can lay the blame on God.

The Lord stood there with his kodak, and was going to take a snapshot of all the ten thousand soldiers, without letting them know it, and in this way he would get an infallible photograph of the moral and spiritual character of every man. God has never changed his plan in this respect.

The souls of men throughout the world, and all generations, are being photographed at such times and in such attitudes as will best reveal the true character of each one; and this is being carried on in such a way that at the last every human being will see that he has manifested his true self, and God will be exempted from all blame, by every human being; and every creature will frankly admit what is in himself.

Those soldiers who bowed down on their knees, and put their mouths down in the stream to drink, in that posture they could not see any stealthy approach of the enemy, and it was a lazy and easy position to be in. On the other hand, those soldiers that only stooped and caught the water in their hands, lifting it to their mouths, they could have their eyes lifted up to see the approach of enemies, and also the posture of their bodies was such as to indicate that they were on the alert, that they were wide awake and diligent, and ready at any instant to make a charge on the foe. In this, they manifested the supreme qualities of vigilant soldiers, and, without being aware of it, they were manifesting to God and to angels their fitness for the very highest rank in service. This is exactly the way God is working among his people. Those believers who are not fully purified, though they are soldiers, yet they have in them the love of ease, the love of self, a proneness of character and disposition, a lack of watchfulness, a lack of understanding, a lack of prompt and swift obedience; and this lack of the baptism of the Holy Spirit is constantly being manifested by them in unconscious ways. They are sluggish in prayer, in testimony, in liberality, in obedience; they do not discern spiritual things, or the approaches of the enemy, and always inclined to take the side of self, or to take the easy side of religion, and in a thousand ways, without knowing it, they avoid the way of the cross, and thus manifest the lack of inward holiness. Those who are accounted worthy to be in the three hundred have in them the very spirit of diligence, prompt obedience, watchfulness, are ever on the alert to see God, and to see the enemies, and to move forward in every duty, in every service, with a promptness, and eagerness, with a courage and freedom of spirit, which is often criticized by weaker and sluggish Christians. True sanctification by the baptism of the Holy Ghost will manifest itself in spite of everything, it will show itself in various ways, and at times of emergency, in such a way as can never be imitated or counterfeited by those who do not have the real grace of that experience.

This eagle band God gave to Gideon were the true elect in the real sense of that word.

The word *elect,* as used in Scripture, never refers to salvation, but always refers to a rank that believers take after their salvation. The word either refers to being sanctified, or to being in the company of the bridehood saints.

Peter says, "That we are elect through sanctification," and urges us "to make our calling," that is, our conversion, "and our election," that is, our sanctification, both sure.

In the Song of Solomon, there is reference to the various companies that are in the kingdom of God, but the bridehood company is spoken of as the true elect, the *choice* one of all others (Song of Solomon 6:8-9). In the fact that there were 300, we see a correspondence with the Trinity, for the number 3 in Scripture is in some way always connected with the three persons in the Godhead. Jesus elected twelve apostles from the world, but when he went up on the mountain to be transfigured, he made a second selection of Peter, James, and John, and those three went up with him to see his glory, corresponding with this 300 that were selected from the 10,000. All these things are still taking place in the history of believers in every generation. There is no partiality in the dealings of God, but he allows everyone to make his own choice, not only in salvation, but also the choice of different degrees of grace, and a choice of what rank each one shall have in the coming kingdom, and then he accepts of the choice that each one makes, and gives them a place, and a work, and a gift corresponding with their spirit of consecration and obedience.

2. The second point in this lesson of Gideon's band is that of their armor.

They had no arrows, or spears, or slings, they had no implements of death in their hands; and this goes to show it was a battle for God, and not on the plan of carnal warfare, but most emphatically a prophetic type of the last battle which Christ and his glorified saints will fight with the armies of Antichrist, without any earthly weapons, but only with the sharp sword that proceeds out of the mouth of the Son of God. Their weapons consisted of trumpets and lamps, and pitchers. Each one was to have a trumpet held in his right hand to blow at a given signal. These trumpets were usually made of rams' horns. The same ram that was slain in sacrifice would furnish the horns that were cleaned out and made into trumpets. The trumpet is a type of the Word of God. Jesus is the ram which was offered in sacrifice, and the same Savior who was offered up as the Lamb of God for our salvation furnishes us with his Word, his horn, his trumpet, and that Word is to be proclaimed in preaching, exhortation, and testimony. The same Sheep whose blood makes an atonement for our salvation is to furnish the ram's horn, the Word by which we are to fight the battles of the Lord.

The Word of God must be apprehended by a living faith as the true inspired Word of God, and not of man. That Word not only becomes the instrument of our salvation by being applied with power to our own hearts and lives, but that Word also is the instrument by which we are to repel Satan and overcome our spiritual enemies. Jesus resisted Satan by repeating the Word of God as spoken by Moses. That same Word which we are to use as a trumpet will also prove to be the sword of the Spirit by which we pierce evil spirits and by which we puncture all false teaching and expose all error. The trumpet will especially be an instrument that will be used in the great tribulation judgment, as we see described in Revelation, by the seven angels blowing their trumpets.

This battle was in a certain sense the judgment day on the Midianites, and so the use of these trumpets at the destruction of the Midianites was a prophetic type of the blowing of the seven trumpets by the seven angels in the on-coming judgment on the nations of this world.

The next instrument of armor was that of lamps. These lamps were types of the Holy Spirit, and just as the lamps were concealed in the pitchers, so the true saints of God are to be armed with the Holy Spirit hidden in their hearts and in their bodies. The lamp furnishes both light and heat, and the Holy Ghost is to dwell within us, furnishing illumination for the mind in the understanding of all spiritual things, and also to supply a divine heat in the heart, the flame of perfect love to God and man.

The human soul is the wick, but the oil and the fire represent the presence and work of the Holy Spirit, acting upon the soul. It is said that John the Baptist was a burning and shining light, but the words really are "A burning and a shining lamp." All through Scripture those two facts of burning and shining go together.

The high priest wore upon his breast, Urim and Thummim. The word *Urim* signifies light, illumination, and the word *Thummim* signifies perfection, a divine fire, the pure heat of perfect love.

The bridehood saints must have the real baptism of the Holy Ghost and fire, not only an illuminated mind to understand divine things, but a heart of fire, and a tongue of fire, to speak forth the words of God with unction, and force, and penetration.

The third instrument was the pitcher that each one was to hold in his left hand. This pitcher was an earthen vessel, and fitly represents ourselves, our earthly human nature. These pitchers were to be broken at a given signal, in order that the light of the lamps might shine forth. How fitly this represents that we must be broken in ourselves and of ourselves in order that the light and fire of the Holy Spirit may shine forth from us.

This truth that God's saints must be broken to pieces is expressed throughout all Scripture and all through religious experience. Everything of self must go to pieces, and everything that is of Christ must shine forth in ever-increasing light and power.

Just as Gideon, the great leader, broke his pitcher that his light might shine forth, so Jesus, our leader, broke his pitcher on the cross, in the crucifixion of his body, in order to let out the great fullness of the Holy Spirit, and of divine life, upon a starving and lost world. And as the three hundred followed Gideon's example and broke their pitchers, so the heroic saints, and especially those who are to make up the bride of Christ, must follow his example and be crucified with him and be broken as he was broken, that out of their broken lives may shine forth the lamps and heat of the Holy Spirit.

It is from the smitten rock that the water flows out, and from the crushed olive berry that the oil flows, and the broken alabaster box that the odors escape, and from the broken pitchers that the light shines forth, so it is from the broken lives of the saints of God that the light and power of the indwelling Christ shines forth both to bless the world and to overflow the adversaries.

3. The third item is the battle. This battle was so arranged by God's providence as to make it a perfect picture of the last battle which will be fought in this world as described in the latter part of Revelation 19. It was also a prophetic picture of the spiritual warfare which the saints of God are waging against wicked spirits in high places. We find in reading the account in Judges that Gideon staged his three hundred on three different hills, forming somewhat of a triangle, while the vast hosts of the Midianites were in the valley below. This position of the hosts is also confirmed by the dream which one of the Midianites had of the barley loaf which rolled down the hill and struck his tent, and this barley loaf was interpreted to be Gideon, showing that Gideon was up on a hill while his enemies were in the valley below.

When everything was ready, about the hour of midnight, when the great host of the heathen were sound asleep, Gideon broke his pitcher and let the light of the lamp shine out, and then blew his trumpet, and all the three hundred followed his example, shouting with all their might, "The sword of the Lord and of Gideon." This was all the fighting that they did. The hundreds of thousands of Midianites were suddenly aroused from their sleep, and looking up they saw the hills all around them filled with shining lights, and heard the loud shouts of Gideon's band, and were thrown in utter consternation, so that in their alarm and terror they drew their swords, and began killing each other until the great majority of them were slain by their own fellow countrymen, and rolled in their own blood, and the rest fled for their lives, and were chased all that night.

In Isaiah 9, there is a prophecy of Gideon.

This is described as the typical battle which will be fought against the armies of the Antichrist at the winding up of the great tribulation judgment.

In Isaiah 9, there is a prophecy of that great battle: "For thou hast broken the yoke of his burden, and the staff of his shoulders, the rod of his oppressor, as in the day of Midian. For every battle of the warrior is, or *was,* with confused noise, and garments rolled in blood; but this shall be with burning and fuel of fire."

The oppressor referred to is the great Antichrist who will despotize this world in the latter part of the great tribulation. This Antichrist is to be destroyed by the brightness of Christ's appearing, and all his vast armies are to be slain in a similar manner to the Midianites. The common translation of verse 5 in Isaiah 9 does not give the real correct idea. The thought is this, the warriors of the Midianites fought with confused noises, and their garments were rolled in blood; but Gideon's band fought with burning lamps, and they had oil in their lamps. The Midianites fought with swords, and shed blood; but Gideon's band fought with lamps and trumpets without shedding any blood, but they shouted, "The sword of the Lord and of Gideon." They did nothing at the beginning of the battle but to shine and shout, and blow their trumpets.

The heathen fought with carnal weapons, but Gideon's hand fought with spiritual weapons, light and shouting.

The same battle is referred to in Psalm 83:9: "Do unto them as unto the Midianites, as to Sisera, as to Jabin at the brook Kison." This verse also refers to the destruction of the armies of Antichrist. According to the destruction in the book of Revelation, the armies of Antichrist in the last great conflict will be spread from Bozrah in the land of Idumea, southeast of the Dead Sea, up along the east of the Jordan as far north as Samaria, and then on the west side of the Jordan the great valley of Samaria up to Mt. Megiddo, under Mt. Carmel, a distance of one hundred and sixty miles, and this is the distance mentioned in Scripture.

According to Revelation 19, Christ will come riding down from heaven on a white horse, and the glorified saints following him on white horses, and they will descend right over Bozrah, and begin slaying the armies of the Antichrist, and ride along over the heads of those soldiers, and slay with the sword of God every one of them up to Mt. Megiddo, or which is called Armageddon, which means the top of Megiddo.

It is expressly said that those armies will all be slain by the sharp sword which goes out of the mouth of the king who rides on the white horse. Just as Gideon's three hundred were on the hilltop, while the enemies were below them in the valley, so the glorified saints will be riding along up in the air over the heads of the armies of Antichrist.

This battle is described in Isaiah 63. It is very erroneous to apply this Scripture to the first coming of Christ, or to the gospel age, for Jesus was never in Bozrah during his earthly life, and there was no *vengeance* in his heart during his sojourn on earth, and hence this Scripture refers to the second coming of Christ, returning with his saints to crush out the armies of the Antichrist, beginning at Bozrah. "Who is this that cometh from Edom with dyed garments from Bozrah? This that is glorious in his apparel, traveling in the greatness of his strength? I that speak in righteousness mighty to save. Wherefore art thou red in thine apparel, and thy garments like him that treadeth in the wine fat? I have trodden the winepress alone; for I will tread them in mine anger, and trample them in my fury, for the day of vengeance is in mine heart, and the year of my redeemer is come. I will tread down the people in mine anger, and make them drink in my fury, and I will bring down their strength to the earth."

It is really pitiful to notice the ignorance of so many Bible teachers, who try to apply these words to the first coming of Christ, or to the gospel, when every word in the passage refers most positively to the day of judgment on the nations, and on the Antichrist, and to the wrath of God which will be poured out upon the beast, and the false prophet, and their soldiers, in the winding up of this age. On the cross, Christ shed his blood, but in this Scripture his enemies will shed their blood.

On the cross there was nothing but infinite mercy, but in this Scripture there will be the vengeance of judgment. Christ died at Jerusalem, but this death scene is in Bozrah, in the land of Idumea, southeast of the Dead Sea. On Calvary Christ laid down his strength, but in this Scripture he brings down the strength of his enemies to the earth. The same battle is referred to in Isaiah 64, where the prophet prays for the time to come when Jehovah will descend from heaven, and wind up the judgment on his enemies. "O that thou wouldst rend the heavens, that thou wouldst come down, that the mountains might flow down at thy presence, when the melting fire burneth, to make known thy name to thine adversaries, that the nations may tremble at thy presence."

These are some of the Scriptures which refer in a special way to that last great battle with the armies of the Antichrist, of which this battle that Gideon fought is a perfect picture.

Isaiah compares the Antichrist to the king of Assyria, and says that he shall smite Israel with a rod for a little while, and then the indignation shall cease, and God will set his anger in the destruction of the Antichrist, and the Lord of hosts shall stir up a scourge for him according to the slaughter of Midian, at the rock of Oreb. And at that day, the burden of the Lord's enemies shall be taken from the shoulders of his people, and the yoke of oppression shall be destroyed because of the anointing (Isaiah 10:24-27).

Another reference is made to this battle in connection with selecting the three hundred which represent the sanctified soldiers in the Lord's army, where the prophet says concerning the last great battle: "Lift up a banner upon the high mountain, and exalt the voice, for I have commanded my sanctified ones; I have also called my mighty ones to execute mine anger, even those that rejoice in my highness, and because the kingdoms of the nations are gathered together against the Lord, therefore the Lord of hosts mustereth his host to the battle, and that the armies of the Lord shall come from a far country, from the end of heaven to destroy the whole land" (Isaiah 13:2-5).

These Scriptures all point to the same thing, that the time is coming when the armies which have the mark of the beast on them, and who are led by the Antichrist, shall be utterly destroyed in a supernatural way by a great sanctified host of heavenly soldiers, fighting with supernatural weapons and gaining the final and everlasting victory over all the enemies of the Lord Jesus Christ in this world. In a spiritual way, God's eagle saints are now engaged in a warfare which corresponds very much with this battle against the Midianites.

Our enemies far outnumber us, both visible and invisible, but if we belong to the three hundred, we are in spirit stationed on a high vantage ground and are fighting in the heavenly places with our enemies below us.

It was God who did the fighting in Gideon's battle, it was God who made the Midianites turn on each other, and slay each other, and it is God who gives us the victory and puts our enemies to flight. We are fighting the battle of faith, as the apostle says, "Fight the good fight of faith." It is our place to follow the Lord Jesus as Gideon's band followed him, and did as he did.

The greatest events on earth have spiritual causes behind them. God brings things to pass in a supernatural way which worldly minded people know nothing about. The weapons of our warfare are not carnal, but mighty to the pulling down of strongholds. "They fought from heaven, the stars in their courses fought against Sisera." This Scripture is still a true word of God, and will receive its last fulfillment in the overthrow of the beast and the false prophet. It is by the baptism of the Holy Spirit that we link ourselves to the supernatural and fight the true battles of God, and it is thus that we have the whole universe and the very stars on our side.

CHAPTER 4

The Molting of the Eagles

THE eagle is a very long-lived bird, and some of them have been known to live over a hundred years even in captivity. When they reach a certain age they shed their old feathers and put on a new growth, by which they renew their strength and their youth. This is referred to by David where he says that the Lord satisfied his mouth with good things, and that his soul had renewed its youth like the eagle's (Psa. 103:5).

This is one of the characteristics in the spiritual life which has been experienced by multitudes of God's devoted saints. Christian biography supplies us with many cases where believers have reached an advanced state of grace in their old age, or after they have passed middle life, and have taken on renewed strength in prayer and spiritual unction, so that in all their inner life there was a renewal of spiritual youth, illustrating the words of St. Paul, that though the outward man shall perish or wax old, the inner man is renewed by the spirit of God. In some cases this has been true of the physical being as well as the spiritual. Mr. Wesley testified that after passing his seventieth year he hardly ever felt any bodily pain or weariness. I have met some rare cases where saintly people have testified that at the age of eighty they felt almost perfectly free from all weariness or bodily suffering. These cases may be rare, but it is especially true that the soul that walks in communion with the Holy Spirit will, in riper years, renew its youth as if it were prophetic of the immortal youth that we are to have in the glorified state.

In the fortieth chapter of Isaiah there is presented a contrast between the natural and the spiritual life: that while in the natural, even the youths shall faint and be weary, and the young men shall utterly fall, yet, in contrast to this, they that wait upon the Lord shall renew their strength; they shall mount up with wings as eagles; they shall run, and not be weary; and they shall walk, and not faint (Isa. 40: 31). The word *renew* in this passage should more properly be change: they that wait on the Lord shall change their strength. That is, change it from the natural to spiritual, from the human to the divine. And this change of strength corresponds to the nature of the eagle in molting its old feathers and putting on new ones. There are three statements in the passage which it will be interesting for us to look into as applicable to our own experience.

1. What is it, then, to wait on the Lord? Waiting on God has a special significance in Scripture, and means far more than to sit down or stand still until a certain moment of time has been reached. We cannot properly say that we are waiting on God until after we have done all of our part in the process. As long as we have failed to meet the conditions of the divine answer, we cannot say that we are waiting. We cannot, in the true sense, be waiting for a railroad train until after we have made all our preparation for the journey, and have purchased the ticket, and checked our baggage, and attended to all the little duties before leaving the station; and when we have done everything and there remains nothing else to do except to step onto the train, it is then that we are in the condition of waiting. This will illustrate our attitude in waiting upon the Lord.

When the penitent has submitted himself to God in prayer, and forsaken all his sins, and righted the wrongs in his past life up to his ability, and forgiven his enemies, and brought himself where he can appropriate God's promises for pardon, it is then that, in the truest sense, he is waiting to hear from heaven, and to receive the response of divine grace that his sins are forgiven, and that he is accepted in Christ, and can realize that he is at peace with God. And when the believer is looking for the gracious baptism of the Holy Spirit, he is not in a true sense waiting on the Lord until after he has made a complete consecration and yielded his whole being point by point, and step by step, to the will of God, and emptied himself of his own self-will, his own plans and ambitions, and laid himself limp at the feet of Jesus, with nothing else that he can do. It is then that he is indeed waiting on the Lord for the Spirit to notify him, in his own heart, that he is accepted, and that his whole being can settle down into perfect soul-rest and pure, boundless love.

Our waiting on the Lord for any answer to prayer does not imply that we are to make God willing to bless us, but it is to bring us into a proper attitude where our inner being comes round into perfect agreement with the divine Word and the divine nature. There are so many things in our nature that we are not aware of, and oftentimes we are not in perfect heart agreement with God though we may not be conscious to say just what the difficulty is. It is the Holy Spirit that searches our hearts and minds, and he knows what it is that hinders; and it is while we are praying and waiting and thinking, that the unseen difficulties are brought to light, or else melt away, so that we come into conjunction with the divine will, where the conditions of God's promises are fully met.

This waiting on the Lord may apply to a great many experiences from the beginning to the ending of our religious life on earth. Sometimes the waiting has reference to our own salvation or sanctification, or healing of sickness, or deliverance from trouble, or success in work, or some blessing for which we are pleading for other people. But let the object be what it may, the principle is the same: that to prevail with God in prayer, we are to reach a place in union with God which he will recognize and sanction as the time for bestowing the answer.

The life of Jesus supplies us with the most perfect example in the world of waiting on God. So many times in the life of Christ he said: "My time has not yet come." His whole being and life moved on a divine schedule, and all his words and actions were timed by the Father's will – and hence the perfection of all his words and ways. When the disciples asked Christ if he would restore the kingdom of Israel, Jesus replied that the times and the seasons were all set by the Father, from which we learn that God does have appointed times for all things that take place, and this must apply to small things as well as great, and to our individual lives as well as to that of the churches or of the nations at large.

2. The second item in the text is that of changing our strength, which corresponds to the molting of the eagle's feathers.

We are to change our strength from that of sin to grace, and from that strength which is natural to that which is spiritual; and from that strength which proceeds from our own will power to that higher form of strength which is inspired by the Holy Spirit. There is most surely a strength in sin, a power in our fallen nature in its energy towards that which is evil. Sin perverts all the faculties and powers of the human soul. It changes the center of gravity from the will of God to the will of self. No man can estimate the power of sinful thoughts and self-will, and a self-centered ambition, until he sets himself to live a better life; and then he finds that he is a slave to his own sins, and that the law of evil is working in him with a tyranny and a force he never dreamed of before. It is this strength of sin working in his soul that is to be changed by the incoming of the new power that will set him free, and institute a new current of strength from some supernatural source outside of him, that will make him a new creature.

In the new birth the believer finds that his whole heart has been changed, and that by the divine life imparted to his spirit through faith in Jesus, he receives a new energy which he never suspected was possible for him to have in this life.

The power that can change human desires and affections is truly a great miracle. It is by this new strength that the new-born soul becomes capable of hating the things he once loved, and loving the things he once hated, and which enables him to go in the opposite direction to all of his previous life. There is no greater proof in all the world of the miraculous power of divine grace than the great change in a real, scriptural conversion. It is this miraculous change which the world cannot understand, and it makes a real child of God a puzzle to the unregenerated mind. It is like putting another law of gravitation into the universe, which attracts bodies in an opposite direction to the old gravitation.

After the believer has gone on a while in the new life he will find his need of another change in his strength, for he will discover that there are forces in his heart and mind which he was not aware of when first converted, that hinder his spiritual progress. No believer will at first understand these difficulties in his inner life, for he is not able to discern deep spiritual truths, and he cannot distinguish within himself that which is purely spiritual and carnal; but he is sadly aware of antagonistic principles within himself. The controlling current of his desire is toward God and holiness and heaven, but at the same time there are other desires which are earthly and fleshly which weaken his moral efforts, and yet he cannot clearly see how to divide these conflicting desires, or to settle what part is of grace and what part is of the old self. There is a mixture in his life of things heavenly and things earthly, of things which are spiritual and things which are carnal.

Man has a three-fold nature of spirit, soul and body. The spirit is the highest part in man's nature, and that part embraces the conscience, the moral life which comes into more immediate touch with God and with divine truth. Then the soul is that part of man which takes in the natural mind, the sensibilities, the reasoning faculty, and through the body and the five senses, comes in touch with the laws of nature. The body, of itself, is simply animal, and under the operation of laws in a similar way to other animals; but the body is the instrument through which the spirit and mind operate.

Now, in the religious life, there are many things in which the soul or the mind act without the co-operation of the deeper spirit and moral nature. There is such a thing as mental religion, which will accept of Bible doctrines and an outward moral life and church enterprises, and be energetic in a great many moral and social reforms, and do much in the way of civic righteousness, where there has been no spiritual repentance, or saving grace in Christ, or real change of heart. There is such a thing as having religion in the soul without having real scriptural salvation in the spirit. There is a vast amount of human religion which does not have in it the life of Christ, or the presence and power of the Holy Spirit. Even after we have been converted or born again, we will find that our religious life is largely mixed with human strength, and that we are unwittingly depending on our will power to reach complete victory in the life of faith. It is here that we learn the need of another change in our strength, by which we are to molt the old feathers of our self life, and take on the new feathers of divine strength which are wrought in us by the baptism of the Holy Ghost. We need to exchange our mixed condition of motives and desires for a condition of heart purity and singleness of eye and oneness of purpose, so that the forces of our moral being are not divided. This is what the psalmist refers to when he prays: "Unite my heart to fear Thy name." Until the soul is baptized in sanctification it suffers with various divisions in the heart, and these divisions are caused by the things of the spirit going one way, and the things of the natural mind going another way. And while this is going on, St. Paul says, "Ye cannot do the things that ye desire to do." To be a strong believer there must be unity in the heart, and all the will so given up to God that it will so one way. This is why we must wait on the Lord in perfect abandonment to his will, and an unlimited consecration to Christ, until that complete change is effected, and the soul, like the eagle, is clothed with a new set of feathers and a new energy by which it can mount up with wings as the eagle: run, and not be weary; walk, and not faint.

We find illustration in the natural world of these various changes of strength in the spiritual life. In utilizing the forces of nature for commercial and scientific purposes, men began by utilizing the blowing of the wind, and falling of streams of water, to move their machinery and propel their vessels. After many centuries of using these natural forces there came the invention, or the discovery, of the power of steam, and so the mechanical force of the world was largely carried on by steam. And in recent years the great motor force has been changing from steam to electricity; so that after the human race has been waiting for long centuries, there has come these changes in the use of various forces, which looks as if the great eagle of the natural world has been molting and taking on new feathers, by which industry and commerce and art have been able to mount up with new wings in the industrial world. These changes of forces in the natural world beautifully set forth the various changes of strength in a new spiritual life.

The religious life often begins in the human feelings and sentiments of natural affection for our loved ones, by which our emotions are stirred ; and if we begin to pray, these sentiments deepen until the conscience is aroused and there comes real sorrow for sin. And as we push on in prayer and believing the promises, the spiritual life takes a still deeper hold upon our inner being, and the spiritual understanding is at last opened, and we discern heavenly things and take hold, as it were, of the invisible world. And as we push on, the power of life becomes deeper in our spiritual mind, and we seem to retire from the outer panorama of the world about us and get more secretive, like men digging deeper in the mines for the hidden treasures of the earth; until, by and by, the whole strength of the Christian life is taken up in the power of the Holy Ghost, and the soul is drawn upward as if the center of gravity had been changed to another world.

All these changes that come in the strength of the soul are reached by waiting on the Lord, by successive steps of meeting the conditions in the divine mind and in God's promises. It is those that wait on the Lord who renew their strength.

3. The third item in the Scripture we are expounding is that of the effects of the baptism with the Spirit corresponding to the results after the eagle molts its feathers.

There are three effects resulting from this great change of power: the mounting up with wings, the running, and the walking. The believer, after receiving the baptism with the Holy Spirit, mounts up with wings as eagles. He is then initiated in a more special way into the supernatural life, and enters the zone of things new and grand and startling in spiritual life and experience. It is a day to date from, when the believer is set free from the old nature, and is lifted by the Holy Spirit into a condition of pure faith and perfect love and cloudless spiritual vision. What great worlds of truth and beauty burst on his vision as he takes his first flight into the upper blue sky of perfect love! His Bible becomes a new book; he looks down from his flight of pure love upon the landscape of his past life and sees all things with such clearness and distinctness! He sees the state of the world, and the state of the visible churches, just exactly as it is described in the Bible. He sees the things of time and the things of eternity in this true light without any cloud on the horizon; his prayers have a spiritual grip in them never known before. There is a directness and a swiftness in spiritual things which are quite startling. Though he has been a Christian for many years, yet, with this mounting up on wings, there is a youthfulness put into every part of his life.

What a wonderful thing is youth and springtime! It is the time of wonders, the period of poetry and discovery and fresh vision. It is an historical fact that great poets always arise at the beginning of a nation's life far more than in the maturity or old age of a nation. Every great poet in the world's history has arisen in the early stage of that nation's history, or at the dawn of some new era of reformation or of letters. What a wonderful thing is youth in our individual life when we are emerging into the manhood of experience! It is then that the whole world is full of poetry, and there is a freshness and zest about everything. There is a period of adolescence – of the bursting forth of youth – which is true of nations, and of churches, and of individuals, and this is true of the spiritual life as well. This is the period of mounting up with wings of eagles.

After a while, the believer who has received the great baptism with the Holy Ghost comes down from his ecstatic flight into the upper sky and touches the earth again, and runs along on his journey without being weary. This is also a perfectly natural effect of the life of perfect love. This represents a more practical and steady-going form of religious experience. He does not fly so high, but has learned to run and to use his feet more than his wings. In this stage of the spiritual life there is a steady, burning zeal for the things of God that urges on the soul with an energy that cannot be well described. The soul is working with the force of a dynamo in the heart, and there must be an outlet to the pent-up energy. There is a zeal for good works, and missions, and religious meetings; or the writings of books, or composing hymns, or singing songs, or starting of benevolent enterprises, or going out to the heathen, or the giving of money, or visiting the sick; a zeal which fairly consumes the soul, like that mentioned in Scripture and applied to David and to Jesus, which says: "The zeal of thy house hath eaten me up."

Then, later on, comes the third effect of the baptism with the Spirit, which is a steady, patient, daily walk with God. "He shall walk, and not faint." The flying and the running stages of experience are just as natural and appropriate in the spiritual life as the developments of youth and early manhood in the physical life.

To walk with God requires more grace and maturity of thought and habit than to fly or run. Young Christians are apt to get impatient with the quietness and seeming slowness of riper Christians. Youth wants to accomplish things with a rush and a speed and a self-effort. To go slow with God is one of the greatest arts in the deeper life of the Christian, and one that it takes a long time to learn unless it is taught the soul by the Holy Spirit. We may read the life of Jesus over and over in the Gospels, but we never get the true insight into his life until it is revealed in us by the Holy Spirit; that life of unutterable calmness and tranquility and quietness and assurance; that life in which everything was measured by a divine regularity like the movement of the sun, moon, and stars, like the rising and falling of the ocean tides, like the orderly movement of the four seasons; that life in which there was no haste, nothing done or said ahead of time or behind time; that life which was so perfect in every form of expression that not one spoken word had to be corrected, not one act was out of place or out of time or out of harmony; that life which moved like the river of eternity, with infinite smoothness and victory. That was the life of God himself, unfolded to us poor creatures through the humanity of the Lord Jesus. We never read that Christ ran in all his life, but that he walked; and yet he was always on time, and nothing was ever overdue. It is into this life that we are to enter and move by the inworking of the Holy Ghost within us. We can never walk with God except as we walk in Christ, and with Christ, and for Christ.

The steady, quiet, slow, mature walk with Christ in the life of faith is the condition of the deepest and most perfect knowledge of divine things. This is the state where the graces all ripen for eternity, and where the soul becomes prepared for that fixed position it is to occupy in the city of pure gold, which is the bride of Christ, in the ages that are to come.

It is a long way from Adam to Jesus, from self to God, from sin to holiness, from the earthly to the heavenly; but the length of the journey does not depend on years as counted by men, but it depends on the rapidity of the steps that are taken, and of the spirit of obedience, and on the willingness with which we comply with divine conditions. Waiting seems to be a slow thing, and yet it is by waiting on the Lord, in the proper way, that the soul meets the conditions upon which it changes its strength, and passes through the various forms of moral and spiritual power, till it reaches the end of the journey in everlasting rest and union with the Son of God.

CHAPTER 5

Principles of Perfection

IN treating of the subject of the fullness of Christian life, there is a very interesting portion of Scripture found in the first six verses of the 6th chapter of Hebrews, where believers are exhorted to proceed from the foundation doctrines of Christian faith, and go on unto perfection. Throughout the entire Bible there is abundant teaching on the perfection of faith and love in the life of the Christian, just as truly as in the completing of a structure, or a building, or the making of a harvest, or of a tree, or of anything in the natural world that reaches its full size or its finished production. In these six verses referred to there are three distinct forms of character. In the first place, we have what may be termed the a-b-c Christian, who has accepted the foundation doctrines of Christ but gone no further. And then we have a description of the apostate, or of one who has turned away from the faith, and put himself into perpetual rebellion against God. And then we have a description of the virtues which constitute the perfect believer.

In order to have a clear understanding of these things, let us briefly analyze the words which belong to each of these characters.

1. Let us notice the a-b-c Christian: The expression, "Leaving the principles of the doctrine of Christ," really means, in the original, leaving the *first words*. Just as we leave the study of the alphabet when we go on to reading, and just as we leave the foundation of a house when we put up and finish the building, so it is in that sense that we are to leave the foundation doctrines of Christ and advance to the knowledge and ripeness of perfection in love.

There are six things that belong to the foundation of Christian doctrine, namely: repentance, and faith, and baptism, and laying on of hands, and resurrection of the dead, and eternal judgment. There are a great many more things in Christian doctrine and experience than these six things, but they form the foundation upon which all the other things rest. Of these six things, two of them belong to the inner life – repentance for dead works, and faith toward God; and two of them belong to the outer life, viz., baptism and laying on of hands; and two of them belong to the future life, viz., the resurrection of the dead, and eternal judgment.

Repentance and faith are the foundation of everything in the inner religious life. Baptism and the laying on of hands are the foundations of the outward sacraments and ceremonials in the church. The resurrection of the dead and eternal judgment are the foundations of everything that is taught concerning the future life. Though there are many more things involved, yet they all rest upon the resurrection and the judgment.

Repentance prepares the way for faith, and it is impossible for anyone to have saving faith in Christ except on the condition of a complete repentance for all their sins. Baptism is an outward sign of inward operation of the Holy Spirit. You notice that the apostle puts baptism in the plural number in this Scripture; this is because the Jews had various baptisms, and even believers who were baptized by John the Baptist were often baptized over again by water after receiving Christ, so that water baptism is spoken of in the plural number. On the other hand, when the apostle says in his epistle to the Ephesians that there is one Lord, one faith, one baptism, he refers to the one baptism of the Holy Ghost, for while there are various baptisms of water, there is only one Holy Ghost baptism.

The laying on of hands was practiced in the early church and is still practiced in the ordaining of preachers and missionaries, and also for the recovery of the sick and the casting out of demons.

With reference to the future state of existence, everything depends on the resurrection of the dead body and upon the decisions of the final judgment. It is these doctrines of the future that furnish the motives and incentives to present faith and conduct.

No one can be a Bible Christian, or form a New Testament church, without the acceptance of these six fundamental doctrines of New Testament teaching. But if these are the only doctrines that are held, the believer will always remain an infant in the spiritual life.

2. Let us notice the terms descriptive of the apostate. There are three words used to designate the character of one that falls away from the Christian faith and remains permanently in that condition. In the first place, he falls away in heart and life; and in the second place, he crucifies to himself the Son of God afresh; and in the third place, he puts Christ to an open shame. These words do not refer to what may be termed backsliding in the ordinary sense of the word, for there, are many who backslide in heart and even in life, who still believe that Jesus Christ is the Son of God, and that the Bible is divinely inspired, and who still hold to the doctrines of Scripture, and many of them repent of their backsliding and are restored to the favor of God, and in some instances they become very zealous in their devotion and religious experience. Here these words refer to what may be termed the apostate, the people who backslide or fall away in such a measure that they become what we call infidels, and utterly deny the deity of Jesus, or the virtue of his atonement, or the doctrines of Scripture. They put themselves where it is impossible to renew them again unto repentance. It does not say that it is impossible for God to save them if the conditions are met, but that they put themselves where it is impossible to make them repent; or, as the word may be rendered, exceedingly difficult for them to repent. Those of us who have had much observation and experience with religious people have met some cases of those who were once in a state of true religious experience, and manifested great zeal in the Christian life, who have not only lost their experience, but gone so far in their backsliding as to become utterly insensible to divine things, or eternal interests and are in such a state of mind

that nothing avails to lead them back to repentance and saving faith.

3. Now let us, in the third place, notice the five things which are mentioned as constituting the perfect believer. These five things are: First, to be enlightened; and second, to taste of Jesus Christ, who is the heavenly gift; and third, to be a partaker of the Holy Ghost; and fourth, to taste the good Word of God; and fifth, to realize the powers of the world to come, or, as the word really means, the powers of the age to come, for the word "world" should be age. These are the different terms used by the apostle to describe the richness and perfection of a true Christian life and experience.

The first word in the process of a believer being made perfect is to be enlightened, which does not refer to education or learning or civilization, but it refers to being illuminated in the mind and consciousness so that the Christian may discern the real state of his heart and inner life.

Christian perfection deals mainly with the inner life; with the motives, intentions, desires, and propensities that spring up from the heart; with the purification of the fountains of experience and conduct. There are multitudes of Christians who are not enlightened with regard to their inner character and who have sinful dispositions and a hardness of conscience and a lack of sensibility to divine things which they are not aware of, and before they can ever become strong Christians they need to have an inward enlightenment so as to clearly discern the defects in their moral nature, and to discover the deep needs of their moral being. Many Christians manifest evil tempers and a lack of sympathy which they regard as only little infirmities, and they never see the magnitude of their shortcomings until they are illuminated by the application of Scripture truth to their conscience. In other words, Christians need to be truly convicted about the necessity of inward holiness, just as really as a sinner needs to be convicted for his sins; and hence, this enlightenment referred to is the first step in the process of the perfection of Christian faith.

The next step to a perfect Christian character is that of gift, for Christ is referred to as "God's unspeakable gift." To taste this heavenly gift implies that we have five senses in our spiritual being, corresponding to the five senses in the body; and just as our five physical senses bring us in touch with the outward creation, so the five senses of our inner spirit bring us in touch with the things of God and of spiritual truth.

When we see our deep need of inward cleansing, it leads us to a life of prayer and of complete consecration until we reach a point where we trust Christ to cleanse our hearts, and it is then that we receive an inward sensation of purity of heart which is denominated the "tasting of Jesus." The sense of taste is a sensation, and we can have a spiritual sensation as to the state of our hearts just as truly as we can have a sensation on our tongue when we taste sugar.

Jesus is not only a being of infinite purity and love, but he has been constituted our Savior, and because he is a Savior he is able, through the ministry of the Holy Spirit, to communicate his feelings and sensations and desires into our souls and our spirits; and it is by this communication of himself into our spiritual being that we become conscious of his blessedness and purity of nature. It is in this sense that we taste of Jesus, and by that taste are partakers of his holiness.

The next step in the process of this heavenly transformation is that of being partakers of the Holy Ghost. The inward sin in the heart prevents the imperfect believer from a full union with the Holy Spirit; but when Christ has been received as a perfect Savior and the soul is purified, then there is nothing to hinder the real partnership of the believer with the Holy Spirit, and it is then that the believer is made a partner, or partaker, with the Holy Ghost. The Holy Spirit yearns to take the believer into partnership with himself, for the accomplishment of all the will of God with the soul, and in carrying out God's plan for his church in the world. By perfect union with the Holy Spirit the believer is taken up into partnership with Christ in a life of prayer, and of good works, as well as the partnership of love and joy, and spiritual power.

Just as the Holy Ghost produced the incarnation, uniting the Son of God with our human nature through the body of the

Virgin Mary, so in like manner the Holy Ghost unites Christ to the perfect believer, and thereby makes the sanctified church a partaker with Christ in all his plan of accomplishing the Scriptures in the saving of sinners and the perfecting of saints, and preparing the way for the coming kingdom, and for God's purposes in the ages which are to come.

The next item in the process of perfecting the believer is that of tasting the good Word of God. It is by the Holy Spirit that the inner senses of the heart are made strong and active. The sense of taste is just as true in the spirit nature as in the body, and under the operation of the Holy Spirit we can taste the good Word of God in a moral and spiritual way just as truly as we can taste food.

The Word of God is different from uninspired books because it is quick and powerful, or living and active, and can be felt when applied to the heart as consciously as material things are felt by the bodily senses. The Holy Spirit can make the Word of God as sweet to the heart as honey is to the tongue, according to the testimony of David in the Psalms, and which has been confirmed by countless examples or witnesses.

As Christians, we need to pray a great deal concerning this matter of our spiritual senses being brought in touch with the Word of God, and the manifestation of divine realities to our hearts. In a short time we are to pass out of these earthly bodies and exist in a purely spiritual condition, and come in contact with unspeakable things in the unseen world: and we will not be prepared for those marvelous and supernatural manifestations unless we are renewed in the spirit of our minds and of our tastes that we may be qualified for those manifestations.

The last item mentioned in this list of the characteristics of perfection is that of realizing the powers of the age to come. The word "world" in verse 5 should be age. There are no less than 35 places in the New Testament where the word "world" should be age, and because of this there has been produced so much misunderstanding concerning the second coming of Christ and the things connected with the coming kingdom.

The teaching of the apostle is that by the Holy Spirit acting on the perfect believer he is brought into a state when he can clearly apprehend the things of the future, and feel strongly the force of those prophecies in relation to the coming age. There are many passages which refer to the power of things to come in their influence on our hearts and lives. It is said of Jesus that he endured the shame because of the prospect of the joy that was set before him. John tells us that if we have the hope of seeing Jesus, we will purify ourselves even as he is pure. These and many other Scriptures indicate that if we are perfect believers we will be mightily influenced by things to come, and especially by what the Bible reveals of the coming of the Lord, and of the next age when his kingdom shall be established in the earth.

Noah lived many hundred years before the flood, which was the first age of human history, but God revealed to him the coming of the flood and then another age or dispensation, which would succeed after the flood; and though Noah lived before the flood, it was by his perfect faith that he felt the coming of future events, and so he realized in his heart the power of the age to come after the flood would take place.

In a similar way, John the Baptist lived in what we call the Jewish age; but he felt the coming of another church age, or gospel age, and he prophesied of the things that would take place in the church age. He knew that Jesus would die and rise again and baptize the disciples with the Holy Ghost and fire, and though he did not live to see those things take place, yet he felt the power of those coming events in his soul. Now, as Noah before the flood felt the powers of a coming age that was before him, and as John the Baptist, living in the Jewish age, felt the powers of the coming things in the gospel age, so we Christians living in the present church age are to realize in a very distinct way the powers of the coming kingdom age, when Jesus shall return and with his glorified saints reign on this earth and chain Satan, and fill the world with the glory of God as waters fill the sea.

Instead of our being fanatics for being alive to the coming of the Lord, we are only getting back to real sober Bible religion by being thoroughly awake to all that prophecy has revealed to us of the coming age and the coming kingdom. In fact, we are not perfect believers according to the New Testament until we are illuminated and intensely alive to the glorious things connected with the return of Christ and his reign on the earth.

There is a tree known as the sugar maple which grows in many sections of the United States and Canada, and this tree is more sensitive to the approach of the spring of the year than any other tree in the forest. In the month of February, while the snow is still on the ground and winter is over the country, there will come a few warm days and the sap will rise in the sugar maple, and if the tree is tapped it will run sugar juice, while all the other trees still have their sap down in the roots and feel no signs of approaching spring. These sugar maples are illustrations in the natural world of those perfect believers who have in them the spirit to feel the oncoming of the kingdom of God. While others are saying that Christ will not come for a thousand years, and multitudes of Christians seem to take no interest in the things of prophecy, and are like those forest trees that do not feel the early approach of spring, and are not aware that the sun is coming up from the southern hemisphere, and will soon bring the heat of summer, so those Christians who are fully illuminated with Bible truth will have those intimations and powerful operations of faith indicating that something great and glorious is about to come into the world, while others who are not Christians or else in a very low state of grace, who are not properly enlightened, seem to feel no intimations of the soon fulfillment of the great prophecies which have been given us concerning the judgments on this world, as well as the restoration of Israel, and the first resurrection, and the manifestation of the sons of God in the glorious age which is just ahead of us.

These are the five great principles which constitute that perfection of faith and hope and love which the apostle urges us to press on into, as a living and powerful experience and life.

CHAPTER 6

Paul's Eagle Prayer

SOME of the most remarkable flights of religious thought and language are expressed in Paul's various prayers. His prayer in the first chapter of Philippians, and the first and third chapters of Ephesians, express the most intense and heavenly experiences possible for a Christian to obtain in this earthly life. Every Christian life is measured by prayer, not merely the amount of prayer, but the intensity, the spiritual insight, the fervor, the sweep, and the perseverance of the prayer. It has been said that prayer will stop sinning, or else sinning will stop prayer.

In these lofty prayers which Paul ofered, that I referred to, there is no reference in definite terms to the work of sanctification, because in reality they are post-sanctification prayers, the heavenly out-breathing of his heart for the fullness of God's life in the soul after it has been purified from all sin.

For many years I have had a desire to write out an exposition of Paul's great prayer in Ephesians 3:14-21. This prayer is away beyond the ordinary ideas of Christian people, and opens up to the devout mind a realm of spiritual knowledge and insight and experience the most attractive and the most amazing for a soul that is thirsting after God. Let us notice point by point the various items in this great prayer.

"For this cause I bow my knees unto the Father of our Lord Jesus Christ, of whom the whole family in heaven and earth is named."God is here called the Father of our Lord Jesus Christ. God is the Father of angels and saints through creation or redemption, and that is effected through his Son, the Lord Jesus. It is this name of the fatherhood of God, the Father of Jesus Christ, after whom every other father in Heaven and earth is named. The word "family" in our English Bible is not the word that Paul used; he used the word *patria*, which means *fatherhood;* just as the word *mater* means a mother, so the word *pater* means a father. The apostle says that every father, or fatherhood, in the heavens and in the earth, is named after God the Father.

The word "heaven" in verse 15 is, in the original, in the plural number – the heavens. The meaning is that throughout all the heavens and all the worlds in the vast creation there are races of intelligent beings that worship God, and that the fatherhoods of all those beings in all those worlds is named after God the Father, and in conformity with his being the eternal father of the eternal and only begotten Son. Everything in the universe goes in families, whether it be among angels or men, or stars, or trees, or animals, or insects; everything throughout the universe goes in families, and the family idea is the one in which all creation is molded. The Godhead is an infinite and eternal divine family or union of Father, Son, and Holy Ghost, three divine persons, of one substance, one eternity, and one glory. And all the families in the universe are in conformity to the glorious Godhead, and all created fathers are named after God the Father. This is the surpassing, lofty conception that Paul presents to God the Father, unto whom he bowed his knees in this surpassing prayer for the saints.

"That he would grant you, according to the riches of his glory, to be strengthened with might by his Spirit in the inner man." The central word in this verse is *strength* to be imparted to the perfect believer. But that strength is to be given according to the measurement of God's riches in glory. There are three kingdoms of nature, grace and glory. The kingdom of nature takes in everything belonging to the creation of the material and mental world in its original form; the kingdom of grace takes in that special plan for the saving of of sinners and restoring fallen men back to the image and union with God, and includes the incarnation, death, and resurrection of Christ and the whole plan of redemption and salvation. The kingdom of glory takes in the ultimate state of glorified beings after having passed their probation, after

the resurrection, and the enjoyment of that full and perfect frui-
tion of the vision of God and the participation in the immortality and bliss and power that belong to the glorified Jesus.

Now just look at the unmeasured wealth in all these three
kingdoms. You see that the riches of glory must exceed all the
riches of the realm of nature and of grace; and it is according to
God's riches in glory by which he is to measure out this dona-
tion of spiritual strength to his perfectly trusting and obedient
children.

The next thought in the verse is that this divine enduement
of strength is to be imparted by his Spirit. The Holy Ghost is
that divine person which brings things to pass, which executes,
performs, and carries into effect all of God's plans and words. The
gift proceeds from the Father himself, through his dear Son, for
every gift that God bestows is included in his Son: and then it
is by the Holy Ghost that that gift, whatever it may be, is made
effectual in the believer.

We are told, in another place, that the love of God is shed
abroad in our hearts by the Holy Ghost, and Paul says that the
Holy Ghost wrought in him effectually and with power: the
same Holy Ghost that applies to our hearts the blood of Christ
in cleansing us is the same Spirit by which we are to be strengthened with might in the inner man, and that Spirit works in us in
co-operation with our prayer and diligence.

The next word in this verse is the "inner man." This word
opens to us another department of knowledge. We are constituted with a body, a soul and a spirit, and it is our spirit which is the
inner man. This inner man of our spirit nature is endowed with
five senses, exactly as the body has five senses, of seeing, hearing,
touching, tasting and smelling. In the case of an unconverted
man, this inner man of the spirit is dormant, dead, unconscious of
the things of God, though his body and his sensibilities of mind
are awake. In regeneration, this inner man of the spirit nature is
brought to life, and in sanctification the inner senses of this spirit
man are clarified and opened up in contact with divine things
and a living touch with the Word of God and the operations of

the Holy Ghost, and the great realities of the unseen and eternal world. But after the believer has been delivered from inward sin, this inner man, with its five senses, needs to be mightily strengthened so as to apprehend the glorious reality and power of divine things. There are countless degrees in which this inner man may receive strength, expansion, inspiration, illumination and power. The soul is greater than the body, but the spirit is greater than the soul, and hence our inner man is the greatest part of our compound being, and the needs of our inner man are more imperative and more lasting than the needs of either the body or the intellect.

"That Christ may dwell in your hearts by faith." This petition is in close connection with the previous one about being strengthened in the inner man, because it is in the inner man where Christ is to dwell upon the condition of our faith. This indwelling of Christ is not a metaphor or a symbol, but it is to be accepted as a literal and positive reality that the Lord Jesus Christ, in his divine personality, is to come and dwell in the center of our being, and reveal himself in fellowship with our human spirit. In order to understand this, we must remember that the Lord Jesus is infinite, the same as the Father, and that his personality can be revealed in an infinite way to an infinite number of his creatures. The rising sun can be reflected in millions of dewdrops, and each dewdrop can receive in itself the entire image of the sun without in any way robbing any other dewdrop, but each drop can take into its bosom the image and glory of the entire sun as perfectly as if there was only one dewdrop on the earth. In like manner, every believer throughout all ages can receive in his heart the entire personality of the Lord Jesus as completely as if there were only one believer on the earth. This indwelling of the personality of the Lord Jesus is not accidental, but it is conditioned upon the intelligent, scriptural faith of the believer, and it is our part to accept of the indwelling of Christ, and depend upon it, and recognize it as a literal fact in our lives, in order that such indwelling may become effectual in our experience.

The next petition in this gigantic prayer of the apostle is, "That ye, being rooted and grounded in love, may be able to comprehend" (or apprehend) "with all saints what is the breadth, and length, and depth, and height." In this verse 17 the word "grounded" really means *founded*, or a *foundation*, such as is made for a large dwelling: *rooted* like a tree, and *foundationed* like a house, in love. In other words, the spirit of the believer is compared to a tree, with its roots running down into the soil of the earth and is compared to a house with a good foundation dug down into the ground. These two thoughts, of a tree and of a house as being likenesses of a righteous man, run all through the Scriptures. David says: "The righteous shall be like a tree planted by the river of waters." And Peter speaks of believers being built up into a spiritual house. Love is spoken of here as the ground in which the tree is to grow, and as the earth in which the foundation is laid for the house. Love is the soil of the heavenly world or the heavenly life, just as the earth is the substance of this material world. Everything that grows in the world grows in the ground or the earth as its basis and support, and so everything that grows in the heavenly world grows out of love as its soil and its foundation.

The prayer is that we may live in the love of God just as truly as the tree lives in the ground, and just as the roots of the tree penetrate the earth and draw out from thence all the substance of its being, so the roots of our soul are to penetrate into the love of God and draw out from the love the sap, the substance, of every part of our life, the flower, the foliage, the fruit, the beauty, the fragrance, and every attribute of our lives. Just as truly as a tree takes every atom of its being from the earth through the roots, we are to live in God; as a fish lives in the sea, as a bird lives in the air, as a tree lives in the soil of the earth.

As a result of being rooted and founded in divine love, we are to become able to apprehend, with all saints, the magnitude of that love. The word "comprehend" in our English Bible should be *apprehend*. The word *comprehend* means to grasp the entirety of anything, but the word *apprehend* means to take hold of anything though you will not be able to put your hand entirely around it. We cannot take hold of the love of God in its entirety and infinite extent, but we can take hold of that love in the Lord Jesus and realize that it is a living fact in our hearts. It is love that gives ability to the understanding, just as human love opens up the natural faculties of the mind; and, as some old writer has said, love makes every man a poet, so divine love – and that is the word used here in the original – opens up the spiritual faculties of the inner man to apprehend the magnitudes of the love of God. Divine love is the greatest stimulant in the universe, and when that love is born into the hearts by the Holy Ghost, it is a divine wine, a heavenly intoxicant, a giant stimulation to all the faculties within us, and nothing else will give us the ability to discover the vastness of God's providences and plans and feelings towards us.

Men have been trying for centuries to find what they call the fourth dimension, but St. Paul had no difficulty in discovering that fourth dimension in the love of God, and he speaks of the breadth, and length, and depth, and height – in other words, he viewed himself as occupying the center, and in every direction – above and beneath, in front and on either side – he saw a boundless ocean of the presence and love of God which could not be measured. And hence he proceeds in the next verse to say, that we might know the love of Christ, which passeth knowledge. The word "know" in verse 19 signifies the most perfect assurance, an inward certainty in our consciousness which cannot be doubted. Some have inquired: How can we know a thing that surpasses being known? It is very simple, for we can know the atmosphere in which we live and breathe, and yet it extends 25,000 miles around the earth, and about 50 miles into the sky, and contains possibilities and attributes which we do not know of, and yet the air can most surely be known, though, at the same time in so many ways, it surpasses all our knowledge. This is just as true of the love of Christ, for there is nothing in the world more sure to a perfect believer than the love of Christ, and yet it is infinite in every way and everything, and has attributes and qualities beyond our understanding.

This leads the apostle to say:"That ye might be filled with all the fullness of God."The more literal translation is, that ye might be filled *in* all the fullness, or *unto* all the fullness, of God. It does not mean that we can contain all of God's love, but that we may enter *into* all the fullness, as we enter into the ocean or into the air. The expression "all the fullness of God" means all the variety, all the attributes, all the perfections, all the various parts of the divine character. There are two words for *all* in the Greek Testament; one is *halos,* which means the entirety of anything, and the other is *panlos,* which means all parts, or all of the number. The word here is *panlos,* which signifies that we are to receive into our nature all the graces and perfections of God up to the measure of our capacity.

The water in the ocean contains gold, salt, iron, sugar, oxygen, hydrogen, nitrogen, and a great many different elements. You can take a thimbleful of that ocean water, and that thimbleful of water contains as many attributes of the sea as the ocean contains. Every part of the ocean is in that thimbleful of water. This is the meaning in Paul's prayer, that our finite spirits are to receive from God all the parts and perfections of his being up to the measure of our nature.

"Now unto him that is able to do exceeding abundantly above all that we ask or think, according to the power that worketh in us." It is impossible to exhaust the provision that God has for us either in grace or in glory. Our asking is measured by our thinking, but as we advance in the spiritual life, our thinking power is constantly increasing, so that we can apprehend far more than we did years ago; and this increase in our apprehension will lead to the increase in our asking; but God stands with an infinite supply ready to meet every increase of thinking or asking, and his ability will eternally exceed all that we can think or ask.

The expression, "according to the power that worketh in us," refers to the power of the Holy Ghost, for he is the divine person that works in us to bring to pass every promise of the Father, and every grace and purpose in Christ Jesus.

"Unto him be glory in the church by Christ Jesus throughout all ages, world without end." It is a singular blunder that in our English Bible one word in the original Greek has been entirely omitted, and that is the word *generations*. The verse should read: To Him (that is, to God the Father), be glory in the church in Christ Jesus, to all the generations of the age of the ages. The reason why the translators left out the word *generations* is because they thought that the word *generation* meant the same as the word *age* or *ages*. The word *ages* refers to periods of time, to dispensations; but the word *generations* refers to races of beings, such as men and angels, and it is a great blunder to confound the word *generations* with the word *ages*. Paul expressly teaches in this Scripture, that there are to be generations, races of beings, like the generations from Adam, that are to be created or propagated in the ages throughout all future eternity, and that these oncoming generations in the future ages are to be blessed, taught, guided and ministered unto by the saints who are now being saved and sanctified. The church of Jesus Christ is to bring glory to God the Father in all future ages, by being ministers to all generations that are to be born throughout all future ages. Thus we see that this gigantic prayer of the apostle embraces every possibility of saving grace and fellowship with God in the present life, and then the prayer extends onward into the age of the ages in the future, so that there is no possible good or glory that is left out.

This prayer soars like the eagle into the upper regions of the sky, with a mighty sweep of vision that stretches to the uttermost well-being, both for this life and for the life to come, not only as to personal salvation, but as to the possibilities of ministering in a glorious way to untold generations that are yet to come.

CHAPTER 7

Creation Groaning for Coming Glory

ONE of the choicest portions of Scripture, revealing the glory of the coming age on this earth, is found in Romans 8:18-27. In the previous verses, the apostle has been speaking of our being the sons of God, and having the witness of the Spirit, and then being joint-heirs with Christ to the great inheritance that he is to receive as the world's Redeemer, and of the part that we are to share in that inheritance, and then draws the contrast between our sufferings in this present life, and the glory that shall be revealed in us when the kingdom has come. The sufferings are of short duration, but the glory will last forever. The sufferings are mostly external, but the glory is revealed in us and also manifested outwardly. The sufferings originate from the creature, but the glory comes out from God.

The apostle then makes a statement that all the creation in this lower world is waiting and looking for the time to come when the sons of God will be fully manifested, and when the curse shall be lifted from the earth, and every part of the lower creation set free from the curse, and share in the glory that Christ has purchased for his people. There are several passages in Scripture which speak of the children of God having presentiments and longings for coming glory, but in this passage the apostle tells us that the lower creation itself is groaning, as if in a mighty prayer, for the glorious liberty of the children of God.

The word "groan" occurs three times in these verses: he says: "The whole creation groaneth and travaileth in pain together until now"; and then he says that we Christians, who have received the Holy Spirit, we groan within ourselves, waiting for the adoption, to wit: the redemption of our bodies; and then he

71

says, the Holy Spirit himself intercedes for us with groanings which cannot be uttered. If we study these three groans in their relation to coming glory, we get a wonderful sweep of vision as to the extent of God's purpose concerning his people, and concerning the renovation and restitution of our natural world in the age to come. Taking the whole passage together, we may regard it as the universal prayer of our creation for the consummation of God's plan of redemption. It is as if God inspired the whole material world, and all the animals and fishes and birds and the human bodies and souls, with one gigantic longing and prayer for the coming of Jesus, and the fulfillment of God's purpose in redemption.

Let us study in detail this threefold groan or prayer for the glory that is to be revealed.

1. The whole creation groans: "For the creature (that is, the lower creation) was made subject to vanity, not willingly but by reason of him who hath subjected the same in hope"; because the lower creation itself shall be delivered from the bondage of corruption in the glorious liberty of the children of God. For we know that the whole creation (or more literally, every creature that has been made in the creation) groaneth and travaileth together until now.

Notice the following items which are mentioned by the apostle: In the first place, all the lower creation has been put under the curse and subject to the law of death not on its own account, or because the lower creatures committed sin, but on the account of man. Everything in this world rises or falls with mankind. When Adam fell, the whole world and everything in it fell with him, and was put under the curse as being identified with Adam's character and destiny. We see in Genesis that when God put the curse on Adam, he also put the curse on Eve, and then on the lower creation, and on the earth itself and then on Satan, the old serpent, so that every part of this world was cursed with man. On the other hand, when Christ redeemed the human race, and purchased salvation for mankind, and gave a promise to deliver the children of God from sin and all the curse and death and every woe, that covenant of redemption embraced all the lower creation, and cattle, and birds, and fishes, and all the products of the soil of the ground and the sea and air; so that when the sons of God are brought forth in the perfect manifestation and glory, all the lower creation will rise with glorified mankind, and enter into the liberty of the resurrected and glorified sons of God. This is the exact promise in verse 21, that the creation itself shall be delivered from the bondage of corruption in the glorious liberty of the children of God.

It is simply marvelous how God has united the human race with this world, with the earth and the laws of nature, and there is a most perfect likeness between man and the earth itself. The world is composed of earth and sea, and air, and so man has a material body which is his earth, and a soul which is his sea, and a spirit which is his atmosphere. And also the laws that govern these three parts of the world are exactly like the similar laws that govern the body and the soul and the spirit. The earth has rocks pervading it as man's body has bones; the earth has trees growing out from the surface as hair grows out from the human body; the earth is full of rivers running all through it as man's body has arteries and veins of living blood running through it; the earth is full of fire and heat, and man's body, in his heart and lungs and bowels, is full of fire, the heat of which keeps the body alive; the earth has volcanoes out of which come the heating fires and gases as man's body has mouth and nostrils for the out-breathing of inward heat and air. The earth is a great, stupendous animal, made like unto man, and man is a microcosm, or a small world, made like unto the earth. God has so united the fortunes of the human race with the earth upon which it lives, that they arise together or fall together, and share in the same fortunes for blessing or for cursing, and this is a proof in connection with the words of Scripture that this world is yet to come forth from its curse and be the beautiful theater for the glory of God in the coming kingdom age.

Another item mentioned by Paul is that the lower creatures are looking with earnest expectation to see the manifestation of the sons of God (verse 19). Have you ever noticed that in the eye of the lower animals there is always a look of expectation? How domestic animals, when they look at us, seem to express in their voiceless gaze a great interrogation point, as if looking for something from us, or in us, which their nature craves? It is a part of the very spirit of creation, a sort of prophetic prayer, a yearning anticipation for some blessing, for some deliverance, to come to them. All the lower creation seem to act and look as if they wanted complete freedom from the condition which they are in. They may not be conscious of all these facts, but God himself has planted the mute expectation into all his creatures, of something better that is to come.

Another item mentioned in the passage is that of the groaning of the lower creatures as if inspired by an unutterable prayer for God's kingdom to come. He not only uses the word "groan" but also the word "travail," as if creation was in birth-pangs for the glorious manifestation of the sons of God, for when the sons of God are manifested then all the lower parts of creation will share in the glory.

It has been noticed by scientific men that every sound in the natural world is in a minor key. The breaking of the waves, the moaning of the wind, the rippling of streams, the bleat of cattle, the singing of the birds; every single sound in the natural world is in a minor key, as if, in spite of all the charms of nature and the beauties of creation, there is still a curse that pervades every atom of the world about us which is expressed in tones of sadness; and it will only be when creation is delivered from the curse that the sounds and voices of the natural world will rise to the glad and victorious major tones of music.

Another item mentioned is that all the lower creation is earnestly looking and expecting to see the manifestation of the sons of God. God made the natural world to be governed by a pure, noble, inspired child of God; but when man fell, he lost his crown, his scepter, his holiness, his wisdom, his beautiful and powerful dominion over all things; and then the lower creatures missed their divinely ordained ruler, and instead of paying homage to man as their rightful lord, they turned against man, to bite, and devour, and rebel against his authority.

God made man to be lord of the lower creation, as is positively set forth in several portions of Scripture, such as, "For thou hast made man a little lower than the angels, and hast crowned him with glory and honor, and thou madest him to have dominion over the works of thy hands; and thou hast put all things under his feet; all sheep and oxen, yea, and the beasts of the field, and the fowl of the air, and the fish of the sea, and whatsoever passeth through the paths of the seas"(Psalms 8:5-8). The lower animals cannot know or worship God because they do not possess a spirit nature such as God has. They do have bodies and souls, and can remember and love and hate, and have many sentiments kindred to those of the human soul ; but they do not possess a conscience, a moral and spiritual faculty, and so cannot come into conscious relation with God; but they can have fellowship with mankind through their faculties of emotion and affection and perception; hence man was made to be their god, and they were made to worship and obey man, as man was made to worship and obey God. When man sinned, he lost his godship over the lower creatures, and they turned against their natural lord. Man, full of sin, has proved himself a brute in countless millions of instances, and far more brutal than the lower creatures, and hence the poor, afflicted animals have been looking for six thousand years to find their natural lord and loving master, the true child of God in his original holiness and power. Had it not been for sin, no lower animal would ever have hurt a human being, but all of them would have been the glad and willing servants to do man's bidding with the utmost docility and affection. Hence the lower creatures are on the lookout for the time when they shall see the sons of God manifested, according to God's original plan. It is true that God has many children in the world, but they are not yet manifested in open vision and power as the sons of God. God's children, in this present life, are kings in disguise, heavenly citizens covered over with infirmities and still under the curse of death and many limitations; but when the resurrection comes and the saints are glorified, then the sons of God will be openly manifested to all the universe, and to all the lower creation, and then the lower animals will be glad to yield perfect worship and obedience to their divinely constituted rulers.

Not a single animal in all the world would ever have hurt the Lord Jesus Christ, for everything in the world felt instinctively that he was the pure, holy, harmless Son of God, and all the demons recognized him as the spotless Son of man, and Son of God, the ruler and judge of angels and of men.

In that passage in the Psalms, where it is said, referring to mankind, "I have said that ye are gods, but ye shall die as the children of men," it refers to this very truth, that God made Adam and the human race to be the gods over the lower creatures, and to exercise perfect dominion over all the lower works of creation. Many think that when Christ walked on the seas he did that only because of his Godhead and as the Son of God; but such is not the case, for the blessed Jesus, in his humanity, had absolute dominion over the works of God, and he could walk on the sea by virtue of the fact of his spotless humanity. If Adam had never sinned he could have walked on the sea, and the fire would never have burned his body, and water could never have drowned his body, and he would never have suffered from the scorching heat of the sun or from cold or wind or lightning, because it is expressly said, in three places in the Bible, that God made man to have complete dominion over all the works of his hands. We never will know how much Adam lost by the fall until we are glorified, and look down from those lofty heights of glorification into the depths of the fall of man.

All these things form a part of that coming glory which is to fill this world when the sons of God are manifested in resurrection splendor and power, and it is for all this that the lower creation is groaning and in earnest expectation.

2. In the next place, let us notice the groaning of the children of God who have received the Holy Spirit. "And not only they (that is, the lower creatures), but ourselves also, which have the firstfruits of the Spirit, even we ourselves groan within ourselves,

waiting for the adoption, to wit, the redemption of our body." It is by an inspiration of the Holy Spirit that we are yearning or groaning for the resurrection. Now it is true that all the heathen world is in a state of groaning, and millions of them are seeking for peace and know not where to find it. Though they have no knowledge or information of the resurrection or the promises of God concerning the future, yet their souls are conscious of being under a curse and they are yearning for deliverance, and we know not to what extent the Holy Spirit may be working in them to produce these longings. But it is in a more definite and scriptural manner that the Holy Spirit inspires believers with groanings for the coming glory.

When the apostle speaks of us having the first fruits of the Spirit, the meaning is, as expressed in other passages, that the gift of the Holy Spirit is the first of all the things that God has promised to his servants concerning the future life and coming glory. In another place the apostle speaks of the Holy Spirit being the earnest, or the first payment, or the first installment, of coming glory, and that, having received the Holy Spirit, he is God's pledge that we shall receive all other things embraced in the covenant of redemption. Our inheritance, as joint-heirs with Christ, includes a glorious resurrection like Christ has, and perfect dominion and lordship over the lower creation, and perfect participation in the joy of God, and perfect exemption from every evil, and perfect possession of every good, and that this completeness of glory is to last throughout all ages without ever being diminished; and hence, he is God's pledge to us that all other things will come to us in due time. This is the import of receiving the firstfruits of the Spirit.

Now, in the next place, it is this Holy Spirit that causes us to groan for our adoption in the resurrection of our bodies. The Holy Spirit does not work outside of the believer in bringing things to pass, but he works through the believer. The Holy Spirit cannot pray by himself and apart from the human soul; but he prays through the believer. Just as the Son of God cannot save the world except by taking a human body and a human soul, and through that humanity make an atonement for the sins of the world, so the Holy Ghost must needs be joined to the believer and live in the believer, in order to inspire the prayers and yearnings and good works and experiences that belong to the gospel of Christ.

And another thought is, that this groaning of the believer for coming glory is not altogether voluntary on our part; that is, we do not originate these longings, but the Holy Ghost takes the initiative with us, and prompts us to yearn for things to come, so that we hear a great cry coming up from the unknown depths of our being, that God would consummate his great plan of redemption. Just as the lower creation groans without understanding the subject, so the believer, under the operation of the Holy Spirit, has drawings and yearnings for coming glory which are beyond his own understanding, and which he does not originate through his own choice.

In the next place, this groaning of the believer, by the inspiration of the Holy Spirit, is for the resurrection in a glorified body. The word "adoption" as used in verse 23 is very seldom understood. We are not really adopted until the resurrection and we come into our full inheritance, though we receive the spirit of adoption after we are regenerated, which is an assurance that we are God's and are heirs to all that Christ has purchased. The word "adoption" was taken from the custom of the Roman people in the days of Paul, which was that when a son of a gentleman reached his majority of twenty-one years, there was a public ceremony and a feast made for him, and the father, in a public way, recognized his son as heir to his estate, and passed over to his son certain possessions which gave him power as a free citizen of Rome, and also authority to act in all matters of business and property affairs. This custom was used by St. Paul to illustrate a similar thing in the kingdom of God, that when the sons of God shall be resurrected and glorified, God will, in a public and universal manifestation, recognize them as his sons before angels and men, and pass over to them their full inheritance of all the possessions which accrue to them as joint-heirs with Jesus Christ, the Son of God, who is the heir appointed to receive all things in the universe. When we are born of God, we become at once heirs to these possessions, and God gives the obedient believer the Holy Spirit to assure him of his sonship and as a pledge that he will possess his full estate in due time; and this is called the spirit of adoption; but the full adoption takes place only when the children of God are manifested openly to the universe in resurrection glory. This is what Paul teaches by saying, in verse 23, that we groan within ourselves because we have the Holy Spirit, and we are waiting for the adoption, which is the glorification of our bodies.

The word "redemption" in the New Testament always refers to the resurrection of the body, the complete consummation of the whole plan of redeeming grace. Also the word "salvation" is often used in reference to the final part of salvation which we are to receive at the coming of the Lord. The Scriptures speak of an initial and of a full salvation, and also of a present and a future salvation; and hence we read of the grace that is to be brought unto us at the revelation of Christ, and of an eternal salvation. When a believer dies and his soul enters paradise, that is not the consummation of New Testament salvation; that is not the perfect state, for as long as his body is resting in the grave he has not received his full redemption; and so we do not enter upon our majority or reach the time of receiving our full possession until our spirits and bodies are united in resurrection glory, and then we reach the consummation of all our prayers and all our groans and all our faith and all the purpose that God has made for us through the redemption of the Lord Jesus.

And this is why the apostle says, in verse 24. "We are saved by hope; but hope that is seen is not hope; for what a man seeth, why doth he yet hope for? But if we hope for that we see not, then do we with patience wait for it." It is hope that runs ahead and links us onto coming glory in the resurrection state, and this hope, by taking hold of future glory and the resurrection, is the power by which we are saved, by which we press on, by which we continue to maintain our life of prayer and trust in this present state. We are saved by faith from our past sins and in our present condition, but if our salvation is not likened unto the future, and if it does not bring us to the consummation of resurrection glory, then everything is lost. Paul says: "If in this life only we have hope, we are of all men most miserable." And again the apostle speaks of hope being like an anchor that enters within the veil and holds steadfast in perseverance until we are consummated in glory. Hence everything in our Christian religion and experience has an ongoing movement, and we are bending forward and like the apostle, pressing to the mark of the prize of the high calling in Christ Jesus; and this is why we, by the Holy Spirit, groan within ourselves, constantly looking and waiting for our glorious resurrection, or else, our glorious translation to meet the Lord in the air.

3. In the third place, let us examine the groaning of the Holy Spirit. "Likewise the Spirit also helpeth our infirmities; for we know not what we should pray for as we ought; but the Spirit himself maketh intercession for us with groanings which cannot be uttered." As I have said before, the Holy Spirit can only groan in conjunction with the soul of the believer. If there were no believers, no salvation, no redemption in Christ, the Holy Spirit, in his eternal oneness with the Godhead, could not groan for anything; but when the Holy Spirit comes into us to carry out the saving grace of God, to apply the atonement, to work in us the will of God, he unites himself with our human spirits, and draws us into fellowship with Christ, and unites us with Christ, and causes the redeeming grace of Christ to become actual and powerful in our hearts and lives.

The Holy Spirit can see with infinite knowledge every detail to the uttermost extent concerning the fall of man and the curse on man and on creation, and he can see the infinite merit of the death of Christ, and also the infinite extent of the glory that is to come, and hence, being a divine person and knowing everything with absolute clearness, he works in us, not according to our vision or our knowledge, but according to God's infinite purpose and glory, and so his intercession and prayer in us is on the lofty scale of divine measurement, and must be beyond our ability to understand or to express; and so the apostle says that he makes intercession for us with groanings that cannot be uttered. If the prayer that the Holy Spirit prays through us was nothing more than our human thoughts and desires, then it could be expressed or uttered: but because it is an infinite prayer to the Godhead for an infinite glory, it lies beyond all our ability to express in words.

According to the Scriptures, the Holy Spirit does everything for the Lord Jesus Christ. We cannot find where the eternal Father, or the divine Son, or the Holy Spirit, act in their various offices for their own selves, but each divine Person seeks the glory of the other. The Father does everything for his Son, and the Holy Ghost does everything for the Son, and Christ does everything for the glory of the Father. Hence the Holy Spirit desires to see the believers in Jesus perfectly sanctified and led on to the full consummation in the resurrection glory, that they may share everything that belongs to the Son of God, and it is this love that the Holy Ghost has for the Lord Jesus, and his desire for the glory of Christ, that he works through the children of God, and groans in them for the final and perfect state of glory which will be the full inheritance of those who are joint-heirs with Christ.

We see that the lower creatures are groaning for the manifestation of the sons of God, because they yearn to see their true lords and masters ruling over them in absolute righteousness and love and wisdom and power, then we see that the Spirit-filled believer groans for his resurrection body and his full estate in open adoption before angels and men. But the Holy Spirit groans for something greater than these things, and that is, for the absolute consummation of every plan and every purpose and every work that belongs to the Son of God.

It is beautiful to notice the rising scale in the reason for these three groans. How the lower creatures want to see the sons of God manifest; and then how the believer wants to see his resurrection glory; and then how the Holy Spirit wants to see the ultimate consummation of everything in the purpose and will of God. It is certainly one of the most extraordinary passages in all the writings of St. Paul. It is at the conclusion of what we may call this universal prayer that the apostle adds: "We know that all things work together for good to them that love God, to them who are called according to his purpose."

CHAPTER 8

St. Paul's Graduation

PAUL was a specimen of the eagle saints – those servants of God who occupy a place in the very front rank of all the people of God. Just before his death, he uttered a valedictory, as it were, a graduating address, in the winding up of his life here, and his entrance into paradise to await the glorious first resurrection.

The spirit of St. Paul made two visits to paradise; the first was when he was stoned to death in Lystra, and his spirit was called up into paradise where he heard unspeakable things, and then his spirit returned to his body to live on, many years, in his marvelous ministry. When he was beheaded under King Nero, his spirit left his body to go to paradise, where he is now resting and awaiting the second coming of Jesus, to be glorified in his resurrection body.

Let us look closely into the wonderful words of this vale-dictory: "For I am now ready to be offered, and the time of my departure is at hand. I have fought a good fight, I have finished my course, I have kept the faith: henceforth there is laid up for me a crown of righteousness, which the Lord, the righteous judge, shall give me at that day; and not to me only, but all them that love his appearing" (2 Tim. 4:6-8). These words cover three tenses, the past, the present and the future. "I have fought a good fight, I have finished my course." This is retrospective of his past Christian career. "I am now ready to be offered." This is circum-spective of what was his condition at that time. "Henceforth a crown is laid up for me," which is prospective of the great glory reserved to the future.

1. As to his past Christian life. Paul groups together the whole of his past life under three forms of speech. The first was

the battle he had fought: "I have fought a good fight" The Christian life is most positively a warfare, not with carnal weapons but with spiritual weapons such as the Word of God, and prayers, and watchfulness. The true servant of Christ is in union with Christ, and has the same enemies that Christ has, consisting of Satan and demons, who are Satan's angels; and then wicked people, treacherous, deceitful human hearts; and then the carnality which the believer has to antagonize in his own self until he is perfect in love. The people of Israel had three kinds of enemies: those in Egypt who were their slave masters, and then those in the wilderness who were their cousins in the flesh, and then the heathen nations in Canaan. Egypt represents the world, and the wilderness represents the flesh, and the enemies in Canaan represent wicked spirits. All these are the enemies that the Christian has to fight. Paul fought this battle to the finish and was triumphant over all enemies.

In the next word he compares the Christian life to a racetrack: "I have finished my course." In many places the Christian life is compared to a racer running on a given track to obtain the crown at the end of the race. There is a special vocation for each believer, and no two Christian lives are exactly alike; for, though the principles of the life are the same in each, yet the outward circumstances and the diversified callings and incidents give to each believer a distinct personal history which is not duplicated in the life of anyone else.

In another epistle Paul had said that he did not fight like a man who was beating the air, and that he was so running as to obtain a crown at the end of the journey.

The third word that Paul used, he compared his life to a stewardship: "I have kept the faith." In this expression Paul compared faith to a golden deposit, a divine treasure that had been committed to him for safe-keeping; and as a good banker takes care of the money that is deposited with him, so Paul, as a good banker, had kept the faith that Christ gave him, inviolate against all heresy and error and infidelity, and had preserved in his heart the one pure faith that Christ had once for all delivered to the saints. There is only one true faith, which is called, in one place, the faith of God, and also the faith of Christ; and this faith, which was in Abraham and in Jesus, has been committed to the true Christian; and the keeping of this faith inviolate against all false doctrine and all unfaithfulness is the test of our probation in this life. Great multitudes of Christians get their faith mixed up with heresy and false doctrine, and fail to preserve the true faith of Christ to the end. This true faith always brings salvation and sanctification and perseverance to the end. Faith is the soul, and obedience is the body of Christian life, and just as, when soul and body are separated, there is a state of death, so when faith and obedience are separated there is spiritual death. Hence faith is both a doctrine and a life. It is perfect agreement with the sound teachings of Scripture, and also a life of righteousness which corresponds with the Word of Cod. Fidelity is the crowning thing in a Christian life, and the verdict at the judgment, "Thou hast been faithful over a few things; I will make thee ruler over many things."

Paul was a victorious warrior and a successful racer and a faithful steward, and these are the three great functions that make up a front rank saint in the kingdom of God.

2. As to the present tense. "I am now ready to be offered, and the time of my departure is at hand." The perfect believer always lives in such adjustment to the will of God as to be prepared for anything that God sends, and to go anywhere in this or any other world where God may appoint. Jesus moved every day according to the program which his Father made for him, and all his acts and words were timed to the Father's will. There is one word which in a perfect way sets forth our adjustment to our heavenly Father, and that is the word "ready." "Be ye also ready." "They that were ready went in to the marriage." At the point of death Paul said, "I am now ready." This is the sublime test of a boundless consecration, to be so adjusted to the Lord Jesus that wherever we are, at any time, we can be so yielded to him as to say, "I am now ready." Ready for service, ready for suffering, ready for worship, ready for prayer, ready for patient waitings, ready to live,

ready to die, ready to stay on earth, ready to enter paradise, ready for the Lord's coming, or ready for long years of labor.

The word "offered" here more literally would be *poured out.* Paul refers to the sacrifices of pouring out water or wine or oil, and he compares his body to a cup and his life to a liquid that was to be poured out on the altar of death. Hence he says, "I am ready to be *poured out.*" The word "departure" is, in the Greek, *analysis:* in fact, *analysis* is the Greek word itself which we have adopted into the English language. The word signifies, *to take to pieces,* and was also used among the Greeks to mean *to take the harness from a horse,* or *take the armor from a soldier,* as well as to take anything to pieces. This is one of the words used in Scripture for death. When the Christian dies he lays aside his armor, or he puts off the harness in which he has toiled; and he is taken to pieces; that is, the spirit and the body are separated. But there is not one hint of annihilation. The miserable doctrine of soul-sleeping and annihilation is utterly contradicted by these words of the great apostle. When the animal is unharnessed he is not annihilated, and when a soldier puts off his armor he does not become unconscious; and when Paul laid aside his human body his spirit did not become unconscious, but entered into that paradise which he had seen before at the time his body was stoned to death in Lystra.

Thus, so far as the present tense was concerned, the apostle was in perfect agreement with God's will and God's providences, and this is the attitude of the perfect believer who is so given up to Christ as to be adjusted to all his circumstances, day by day, depending not on his circumstances, but depending moment by moment on the Lord Jesus for all things.

3. As to the future. "Henceforth there is laid up for me a crown of righteousness, which the Lord, the righteous judge, shall give me at that day, and not to me only, but unto all them also that love his appearing." Apart from the future, everything would break down and give way. If there be no resurrection from the dead, Paul says, our life is vain, our hope is vain. Paul says his crown is laid up for him, and that he would receive it "at

that day," that is, the day of Christ's second coming. There is not one single word in all the Bible about anyone getting his reward at the time of death, but every single Scripture on the subject teaches that the righteous will get their rewards at the second coming of Christ and not before. In speaking of the death of a Christian, people often say that he has gone to his reward; but the Bible denies it, and it only shows how many common expressions there are among Christians that are not found in the Bible. The Scriptures always speak of the death of the righteous that they have entered into rest, that they are gathered to their people, that they have gone to be with Christ, that they have entered into paradise, that they have ceased from their works; but there is not one word about getting their reward till Jesus comes. It was said to Daniel that he should rest, and get his reward at the end of the days. Jesus says: "I come quickly, and my reward is with me." And so the crown that St. Paul is to wear through the glorified ages is now hung up in the heavenly places waiting for him to get his resurrection body, and receive his judgment at the seat of Christ, and then Jesus will give him the crown, and he will take his place in the front rank of the great saints in the kingdom of God.

Some years ago a very saintly man in humble life, dreamed that he went to heaven and saw a great factory where angels were making crowns for the saints, countless thousands of crowns of all sorts and different sizes and shapes and of almost infinite variety in their make-up and degrees of purity and splendor. He dreamed that his guide told him that when a man became a Christian the Lord sent an angel to measure his head, and have a crown prepared for him that would fit nobody in the world except that one person, and that if that Christian would carry out the life work that God had planned for him he would get the crown, and that if he failed to do all his work the crown was changed.

We are saved by faith, but we are rewarded according to our works. We have salvation now through faith, but our crown has connection with our life-work. We are to earn the crown before we die, but receive the crown at the coming of the Lord.

The Bible speaks of a crown of life, and a crown of righteousness, and a crown of glory. I do not think we ought to say that these different words represent three different crowns, but they are different terms which refer to the same crown which we are to receive. The crown of life may refer to a crown for having lived a godly life, or a crown wrought out of the life of Christ; a crown of righteousness implies a crown for righteous actions, not only a crown for having a righteous heart, but a crown for righteous activity in thought and prayer and will and love and action and obedience, and the crown will correspond exactly to the amount of righteousness; a crown of glory implies the crown of glorification belonging to a resurrected and glorified body, a crown of glory in distinction from a natural crown or a crown of grace. This crown will be literal and real. John saw the elders in the Revelation wearing crowns of pure gold, and I take it that the words mean exactly what they say. Gold is the finest metal that has ever been found in the material creation, and the city of the New Jerusalem is made of pure, transparent gold, which will be a literal fact and not a metaphor. The people who teach that the crown is only a metaphor or an illustration are apt to have a religious experience of the same order; in other words, they have only a metaphorical religious experience, a metaphorical conversion, and a metaphorical sanctification, and only a typical baptism of the Holy Ghost, and so they have nothing but a symbolic religious life without any powerful reality, and are looking for nothing but symbolic resurrection and a symbolic second coming of the Lord, and all their religious life is a shadow and a sham.

The crown that the glorified saint is to wear on his head will have in it those things which indicate the life he has lived, the work he has done, the measure of his piety; and that crown will indicate his rank in the kingdom of God, and everyone that looks on his crown will be able to see at once his rank in the kingdom of heaven, and the measure of his rewards as well as what has been the peculiar state of his life of faith in the past.

The apostle unites himself with other saints and speaks of other believers receiving a similar crown, especially those who love the appearing of the Lord Jesus. To love the appearing of Christ is something more than to love Christ in the ordinary sense of that word. It means not only to love Christ as a Savior, and love his character, and to love his church and his gospel, but, more than all these, to love his person, to love him in his glorified body, to love him as a coming King to rule over the earth, to love him the way he appeared to Daniel and on the Mount of Transfiguration, and in his resurrection glory. This form of love makes Christ a more vivid reality than is experienced by ordinary believers. It makes Christ a glorious, bright reality to the soul, and this is what we need to qualify us to see his face.

In all the Bible, Paul is the only one that has left us a testimony at the close of his life, and God has used him as a sample of the eagle saints who have, by grace, prepared themselves for the flight, either into paradise, or for the flight of the translation, when Jesus gathers his people to himself in the sky.

CHAPTER 9

The Flight of the Eagles

THE second coming of Christ will have two stages to it. The first stage is called the rapture, or the catching away, when Christ will appear in the sky and resurrect the dead saints and catch away the living saints and gather them unto himself. And the second stage is called the revelation, when Christ will return after the tribulation judgment, and bring his glorified saints back to the earth, and chain Satan, and set up his kingdom on the earth. The Greek word *parousia* is used in connection with the rapture, and the Greek word *apocalypse* is used in connection with his return in open glory with his glorified people. There are two sets of Scriptures concerning the second coming of the Lord. One set represents the rapture, and other portions of the Scripture represent the revelation, and it is impossible to understand these different Scriptures except they be explained in connection with these two stages.

There are two passages which speak of the catching away of the saints as the flight of eagles that are gathered to the crucified and glorified body of Jesus. See Matt. 24 :28, and Luke 17:37: "I tell you, in that night there shall be two in one bed; one shall be taken, and the other shall be left. Two shall be grinding together; the one shall be taken and the other left. Two shall be in the field; one shall be taken, and the other left." "And the disciples said unto him, Where, Lord?" that is, where will they be taken? "And he said unto them, Wheresoever the body is, thither will the eagles be gathered together."

Many teachers try to interpret this Scripture as referring to the destruction of Jerusalem, and the coming of the Roman legions like eagles to devour the dead body of Judaism, but such interpretation is absolutely foreign to the Scripture, for in the entire passage there is no reference to Jerusalem or to the Roman armies; but it is expressly in connection with the second coming of the Lord, and to the fact that those people who are prepared to meet Jesus will be called away from the earth, and those who are not prepared to meet him will be left behind. All the Scriptures that set forth the second coming of Christ have been, for so many centuries, misinterpreted by being treated only as metaphors and spiritualized away, that it is difficult to get the church back to the interpretation of Scripture as understood by the early disciples in apostolic times.

We have seen, all through Scripture, a class of saints that are designated as "eagles" because of their being in the front rank of the Lord's people, and occupy a place in the spiritual kingdom of God compared to the place that eagles occupy in the kingdom of birds.

In the second place, reference is made by our Lord to the fact that eagles will gather around the body of some animal which they have slain, and that they will feed on that body. Eagles do not feed on carrion, but they eat the fresh meat of some animal which they themselves have killed, and they will not touch any decayed flesh, except to prevent starvation. Both in the passage from Matthew, and also from Luke, this reference is made about the eagles feeding on a slain body. It is certainly true that Christ was crucified by the human race, and it was our sins that nailed him to the tree, so that in one sense we are all partakers in slaying the blessed Son of God. This same body of Christ that we have slain by our sins, is the very food on which we live, for we are saved by his death, and Jesus emphatically tells us that except we eat his flesh, and drink his blood, we have no life abiding in us. The crucified and glorified body of Jesus has been the vital source of nourishment to all believers in all generations; and when that glorified body descends from the Father, and appears in the sky, those saints who have been feeding on that body, and who will continue to feed upon it, will be called up to meet that blessed body in the air; and the catching away of the living saints is compared to the flight of eagles.

When the Roman soldiers destroyed Jerusalem, there was no such thing as two being in bed together, or cooking their breakfast together, or at work in the field together, and one was called away and the other left; hence it is absurd to apply this Scripture to the destruction of Jerusalem, and it can have no meaning in the world except as applied to the translation of living believers at the time Jesus comes in the air to gather his saints unto himself.

In the third place, the Scriptures furnish us with some types and samples of the translation of the saints and the flight of the eagles, and such translations have taken place just before great judgments were poured out. Just before the flood, Enoch was translated, called away from his family and associates on earth and instantly removed to some place in the heavenly world. Also just before God's judgments on the ten tribes of Israel, in their captivity by the Assyrians, God translated the prophet Elijah, and in a moment of time he was called away from his companion and servant, Elisha, and his other brethren of Hebrew prophets; so that, in a moment, one was taken and the other was left. In both of these cases the translation took place just before severe judgments, and in this respect they are samples of the translation of the prepared saints just before the setting in of the great tribulation judgment which is to come on the entire world.

Another type of the translation of the saints is furnished in the case of Moses, who went up in Mount Sinai to meet God, and took with him seventy of the elders of Israel who were separated from the congregation, and gathered up into the mountain and had a vision of God, and ate and drank in God's presence, while all the nation of Israel remained below. "Then went up Moses and Aaron, Nadab, and Ahihu, and seventy of the elders of Israel; and they saw the God of Israel; and under his feet was a paved work like a sapphire stone; and they saw God, and did eat and drink!" (Exodus 24 :9-11). This was a prophetic sample of what is to come in the translation of the saints, "when one is taken and the other left."

Another type and sample of the flight of the eagles is given at the time of the transfiguration, when Jesus selected three disciples, Peter, James and John, and separated them from the other disciples and took them up to the mountain top, and was transfigured before them, giving them an appearance of himself just as he will be seen at his second coming in glory.

These instances agree in their teaching, and show precisely what is to come at the time of the rapture.

In the fourth place, the rapture will not he pre-announced, but will come suddenly, without any preliminary notification, and hence may take place at any time: and this is why Jesus commanded all his disciples to watch, for he would come at a time when people were not expecting him.

Now, on the other hand, before Christ returns from heaven with all his glorified saints, he will be heralded by the two witnesses that stand up against the Antichrist in the judgment period. In this respect the first coming of Christ supplies us with an exact sample. The birth of Christ was the first stage of his coming, and it was not announced beforehand, and he came in the night, and unannounced, in a private way, at a moment when the world was not expecting it: and only after his birth was it made known, and then to nobody except a few prepared ones who were to receive the truth. On the other hand, after spending thirty years in retirement, he suddenly appeared in open manifestation at the Jordan, to be baptized by John, and that open appearing was heralded six months beforehand by John the Baptist. Thus we see the first stage of his coming in Bethlehem was secret and unheralded, but the second stage of his coming in open manifestations at the Jordan was heralded by John. This is exactly a likeness of what will take place at his second coming, for the first stage in his coming will not he heralded, but in an unexpected hour he will come in the sky to gather the eagle saints unto himself. But after a period of thirty or forty years, when the tribulation judgment has passed, he will be heralded by the prophets Elijah and Enoch, who will be the two witnesses against the Antichrist, and they will fore-announce to all the world the coming of Jesus with all his saints in great glory to destroy the Antichrist: to chain Satan, and set up the kingdom of God in the whole world.

Now let us notice the fifth point in connection with the flight of the eagles at the time of the translation and the first resurrection. The change that will take place with the righteous at that time will be far beyond all our comprehension in our present state. In this present life, Jesus compares his children to chickens. Referring to his people who were living in Jerusalem, and who were about to be destroyed by the Roman soldiers, he said, "O Jerusalem, how often would I have gathered thee, as a hen gathereth her chickens under her wings, but ye would not come unto me, and now desolation is coming upon you." How true to the facts in the case it is that Christians in this life are like little chickens, and Satan is like a hawk watching to pounce on them and destroy them, how poor, how helpless the real saints of God are in relation to this present world and to their enemies and their multiplied trials and infirmities, exposed to a thousand temptations and snares, visible and invisible, so that they need fly constantly under the invisible wings of the omnipotent Jesus for shelter and safety. But this illustration about chickens refers only to this present life. On the other hand, all the Scriptures that refer to the righteous as eagles are in connection with the saints in power and glory, when they will be lifted into an immortal state, and set free from all trial and trouble and weakness of the flesh, and be transported to immortal glory equal to the angels.

In order to understand any word in Scripture, we must take it in connection with its proper situation and setting in relation to other things. For instance, Jesus told Peter that he was blessed, and that flesh and blood had not revealed the deity of Christ to him, but that his Father in heaven had revealed to Peter the true Messiahship of Jesus. Now, it was hardly an hour after this that Jesus called Peter Satan, when Peter reprimanded Christ about dying, and Jesus said, "Get thee hence, Satan, for thou savorest not the things that are of God." Now, you see, you must take words in their proper relationship. When Peter confessed his faith in the divinity of Christ, he was speaking by the Holy Spirit as a believer; but, on the other hand, when he reproved Christ at the thought that Christ must die, he was speaking simply out of his natural, carnal, human reason. The faith of Peter was of God, but the carnal reason of Peter was of Satan. And there are many other things in the Bible that can never be understood except by taking them in their proper relation. Hence, as poor, weak servants of God in the present life of trial and suffering, we are like little chickens, running to the mother hen for shelter. But, on the other hand, when Jesus comes and the living saints are suddenly glorified and translated, they will be like great, powerful eagles, soaring to the loftiest heights in the sky and absolutely victorious over every difficulty and every adversity and every limitation and infirmity connected with the flesh.

According to Scripture, nothing will be more instantaneous than the catching away and glorifying of the saints at the rapture. Paul says: "We shall not all sleep, but we shall all be changed in a moment, in the twinkling of an eye, at the last trump; for the trumpet shall sound, and the dead shall be raised incorruptible, and we shall be changed ; and this corruptible shall put on incorruption and this mortal shall put on immortality" (1 Cor. 15:51-53).

And again: "We which are alive and remain unto the coming of the Lord shall not prevent" – that is, go in advance of – "them that sleep; for the Lord himself shall descend from heaven with a shout, with the voice of the archangel, and the dead in Christ shall rise first; then we which are alive and remain shall be caught up together with them in the clouds, to meet the Lord in the air; and so shall we ever be with the Lord" (1 Thes. 4:15-17).

Nothing can be quicker than the twinkling of the eye, and yet just as suddenly as we wink the eye so suddenly will come the great change from our present condition into that of unspeakable glory and immortality. This shows that it will not be in the line of natural law or evolution or any progressive change like the development of species in the animal kingdom, but the instantaneous act of an omnipotent God, who speaks and it is done. This is contrary to all nations of men and all human philosophy, and belongs to things revealed by the Holy Ghost and not to things sought out by human discovery.

The resurrection of the dead saints will take place first, and then, immediately after, the righteous who are living will undergo a change which will be equal to death and to resurrection, and then both the resurrected saints and the transfigured ones will be caught up together in that sublime flight from the surface of this earth to the upper regions of the sky, where they will meet the glorified Jesus, and see him in his infinite splendor and holiness, and hear his dear, sweet, audible voice, and be led by him to some place in heaven where they will give in their account to him, and be judged in order to receive their proper rewards, and each one be allotted his place and rank in the kingdom of heaven, and where the crowns will be given and rewards will be given. This great divine change will be beyond the region of all human science or earthly knowledge or experience thus far known in the history of mankind.

In concluding this chapter·, I want you to notice the connection between the latter part of the third chapter of Revelation and the first part of the fourth chapter. To the last of the seven churches John says: "To him that overcometh will I grant to sit with me in my throne, as I overcame and am set down with my Father in his throne" (Rev. 3:21). This is the last reference to the church in the gospel age, and the word "church" does not occur after this chapter clear on to the millennium in chapter 20; and we have in this verse a hint at the translation of the saints when they arc called up to sit with Christ in his Messianic throne. Now notice that in the next verse, in chapter 4: "There was a door open in heaven: and a voice like a trumpet said, Come up hither." And immediately John was in spirit, and the word does not mean that he was in Holy Ghost, but the original word signifies that he became like a spiritual being, like a glorified saint, and saw a throne, which was the Messianic throne and not the eternal throne of God the Father; and around that throne he saw twenty-four other thrones (for the word "seat" is, in the original, "throne"), and on these twenty-four thrones he saw the glorified elders sitting, clothed in white raiment. And then he saw, in the center of the throne and round about the throne, four living creatures, one like a lion, another like a calf, the third like a man, and the fourth like a flying eagle (Rev. 4: 1-7). Now, here we see another reference to the eagles, showing that the victorious saints, who were the overcomers in the last of chapter 3, were, in chapter 4, caught up through the open door in heaven where they saw the Lord on his throne, and where they had thrones in companionship with the Lord Jesus; and those saints who were like eagles had taken their flight and were now associated with the Son of God in his royal authority, taking part with him in administering the dispensation judgment upon the world.

CHAPTER 10

The Prayers of All Saints

THERE will be a great many things that will occur after the saints are caught up to meet the Lord and pass their judgment and get their rewards, before they return with Christ as a glorified army back to the earth to govern the world with Christ through the thousand-year kingdom period.

The bridehood saints will be caught up through the open door into heaven, as described in Revelation, Chapter 4. The word "church" is not used in the book of Revelation between chapters 3 and 20, because all of those chapters are filled with the events that will occur during the great tribulation, and at that time the true church will not be on the earth, but glorified and up in heaven.

The tribulation judgment will likely last for forty years, corresponding to the forty days and nights it rained at the time of Noah's flood. The Antichrist does not arise until toward the close of the great tribulation, so we must not confound the time of the Antichrist as being the same as that of tribulation judgment.

Soon after the beginning of the great judgment on the living nations, there will come a great revival, which is described in the seventh chapter, during which time the storms of judgment are held in check by the four angels on the four corners of the earth; and after that great revival, in which one hundred and forty-four thousand of Jews are saved as the first-fruits of the restoration of Israel, and also a countless number will be saved from among the Gentiles, then will occur an event of great significance, when the Lord Jesus, as High Priest of his people, will collect all the prayers of all the saints of all ages, and present them to the Father for the great consumption of the history of God's people, and the final answer to all their prayers, both in glory to the saints and in judgment on the wicked. This event of offering the prayers of all the saints is described in Revelation 8:1-5. "And when he had opened the seventh seal, there was silence in heaven for the space of half an hour. And I saw the seven angels which stood before God; and to them were given seven trumpets. And another angel came and stood at the altar, having a golden censer: and there was given unto him much incense, that he should offer it with the prayers of all saints upon the golden altar which was before the throne. And the smoke of the incense, which came with the prayers of the saints, ascended up before God out of the angel's hand. And the angel took the censer, and filled it with fire of the altar, and cast it into the earth: and there were voices, and thunderings, and lightnings, and an earthquake."

This consummation of all the prayers of God's people will be manifested at the opening of the seventh seal. The events in the seventh seal include the seven trumpets, and the seven vials of wrath, and run on to the end of the tribulation judgment, and terminate at the destruction of the Antichrist and the chaining of Satan.

There will be some deep relations between the prayers of the saints and the ministry of the seven archangels referred to in this passage, for inasmuch as those angels have been actively engaged for six thousand years ministering to the human race in various capacities, they have had much to do with the lives and destiny of God's people, and so it is fitting that they should appear before the throne, and be witnesses to the great consummation when the prayers of the saints receive their final answer.

These seven angels stand before God, and are called the angels of God's presence, but more literally the angels of God's face, and Jesus tells us of certain angels that do always behold the face of our Father in heaven. The names of these seven archangels are not all given in the Bible, but from the writings of ancient Jews which have come down to us in Apocryphal books, we learn their names, and also an indication of the various ministries that they perform. Their names and official ministers are as follows:

Uriel is the archangel that superintends all wars and conflicts of nations.

Raphael is the angel that presides over the spirits of men.

Raguel is the angel that superintends various punishments dealt out to nations and men.

Michael is the archangel that has special guardianship over Israel and the relations between Israel and other nations, as referred to in the book of Daniel.

Sarakiel is the angel that presides over transgressions and various degrees of disobedience.

Gabriel is the archangel that has supervision over the church, and over paradise, and the spirits of the righteous dead. Hence it was Gabriel that announced the birth of John the Baptist, and announced the birth of Christ, and likely the one that appeared to Cornelius, and that will blow the trumpet for the first resurrection.

Ithuriel is the angel that presides over frauds, deceptions and intrigue.

These seven archangels rank the highest of all creatures in the government of God.

The church of the firstborn, which make up the bride of the Lamb, will sustain a closer relation to the Son of God in love and in domestic union and in the outworking of the plan of redemption than these seven angels, because we must distinguish between those relationships which are of a domestic order or belonging to the family ties, and those which relate to the imperial administration of universal government. For example: Our president has a body of men united with him called the cabinet, who are the heads of the various departments of government, and they make up the official body of the president, and take the highest rank of any citizens of the nation next to the president; but the wife and children of the president are more closely related to him in domestic affairs and in family relations. This will serve to illustrate the difference between the archangels being the highest creatures in the universal government of God, but that those saints who make up the bride of Christ are more intimately united to God in ties of redemption and love and family organism.

In the passage we are expounding, after the mention of the seven archangels, there is mention of "another angel" that had the golden censer, and that offered the prayers of all saints. This "other angel" is the great High Priest, the Lord Jesus himself, and there are several passages in which Christ is spoken of as "another angel," and in all such passages he is described by the attributes and functions of the High Priest, the Son of God.

When we study the progress and destiny of the human race, we must remember that it has one history in the natural life, which is the history of the fallen race of Adam, and which has never shown any improvement, so far as moral character goes, from the days of Cain down to the present hour: and all of this history, in every detail, and comprising the life of every individual, has been recorded and preserved by the angels of God, who have kept the record of all human affairs with infallible precision. Then there is another history of the righteous and comprising all the operations of divine grace upon human beings, which includes the various revelations God has made to men, and the operations of the Holy Spirit upon human beings, and all the instances of repentance and faith and salvation and good works and growth in grace, and the history of all the prayers that have ever been offered in sincerity and in truth by all the Lord's people in all generations.

There are some points in connection with the prayers of all saints that we ought to fasten in our minds, in order that we may see the magnitude of that event when this Scripture will be accomplished, and when there will be the perfect and final answer to every prayer that has been offered in a manner acceptable to the Lord.

1. Prayer is a fundamental part in the history of the human race, and was arranged for by the Almighty in his original plan of the creation. Foolish and ignorant men that know nothing of God, and almost nothing of his inspired Word, look upon prayer as a fanaticism, or as something that lies outside of the realm of

law and the government of the world. When God formed the universe he instituted the law of prayer as being just as fundamental as any other law in creation. We speak of natural law, but no such term is used anywhere in the Bible, for in the inspired Scriptures every such thing as we designate by "natural law" is attributed to God, as a mode of the working of his power and wisdom in all things. According to our way of speaking there are certain laws which operate in the natural creation such as gravity, light, heat, motion, cohesion, repulsion, electricity, and similar forms of power and force. Then we speak of certain laws operating in the soul or mind, as love, hate, memory, decision, cause and effect, and the various relationships of creature to creature, and the various developments in the progress of society. But we have revealed in Scripture another set of laws which outrank those in the material or in the mental world, and they are those laws which operate between God and the soul.

God has planned in all the creation to deal with men according to their desires and choices and conduct, and he has made certain rules by which he will act, upon certain conditions that his creatures may conform to. Nothing in all the Bible is more absolutely revealed than the fact that God will answer prayer, that he will do certain things upon the condition of men presenting their requests to him in the way that he prescribes, and in the spirit which he dictates.

When we pray to the infinite and eternal God in the name of his only beloved Son, and in the spirit of complete submission and faith and hope, we are acting in agreement with a divine law which is higher than any other law that operates in the realm of nature. God is certainly greater than his works, and the welfare of the souls of men is greater than the mere display of material things. So that prayer is a higher law than the forces that scientists deal with, and just as, when a king takes a journey through his kingdom, every railway train must be side-tracked in order to make way for the royal train, so every law in the material world must, if necessity so requires, be set aside to make way for the answer to those prayers which are more dear to God than all the things of a material nature.

2. In the next place, prayer is the highest power in the gift of mankind. On the divine side the law of prayer outranks all other law; so, on the human side, prayer enables man to exercise the greatest power which it is possible for a man to have. If by prayer, in conformity with the revealed will of God, we can move God to do things which he would not otherwise do, it is certain that we thereby have a power to accomplish results greater than we have in any other direction. After we have enumerated all the powers of the human body, and the human will, and all the devices of invention and art, and then added to that all the power of personal magnetism and influence, and all the power of the united gifts and talents with which we may be endowed if, above all these things, we can persuade God to do things for us, and in us, and through us, which would never be accomplished except on the condition of prevailing prayer, you see at once that here is a force that is supernatural.

There can be no greater power given to a human being than that of prevailing with God to do things which neither man nor angel could otherwise perform. It is certain that prayer moves the arm that moves the world. The weakness of man is beyond all our comprehension, and when we look at ourselves as disconnected from God, nothing can be more hopeless or helpless. And yet while our weakness in and of ourselves is simply infinite, yet God has given us his only begotten Son, that by his crucifixion and death and resurrection, we may present our petitions in his name, and in union with his merit as a Savior, and thereby cause miracles to be wrought in a great many directions, so that it is like taking hold of the arm of Omnipotence, and using that arm to accomplish things needed for ourselves, both in this life and in the life to come.

3. True prayer is immortal, and does not belong to those things which die and pass away, because it originates in the immortal spirit of man, and under the guidance and inspiration of the Spirit of God, and also it belongs to the immortal world,

and not to the realm of material or animal things. It is by prayer that we take hold on God, and get visions of God, and understanding of his revealed Word and will, and get insight into his providences, and besides it is by prayer that we form a character in conformity with the image of Christ.

Every man's character depends on his prayers. It will be seen, at the final judgment, that all holy character will be in exact conformity to what has been the prayer life of the individual. There is a history to prayer which is so interior and spiritual that we ourselves are not able to analyze it, or to mark its various degrees, and it would take the intelligence of an angel to write out the history of the prayers of God's people, and doubtless it is this that will be by the archangels manifested at the time that the powers of all saints are brought to their culmination and completion.

4. The history of prayer has been interwoven with the history of the world from the beginning, and none but God can know how all the history of the world, and the various nations and families and individuals have been connected or modified or molded by the prayers of God's people. What would the history of the human race be if every true prayer of the righteous should be taken out of it? In order to form a conception of this picture, let us suppose another one, by asking, what would the history of the world be if the Bible were entirely taken out of it? Suppose that not one line of the inspired Scriptures had ever been made known or revealed to mankind, what would have been the condition of the world? In order to eliminate the Bible entirely from the world, we must not only destroy every copy of the Bible that has ever been written or printed, but we must remove every quotation from the Bible that has been put into every other book in the world, and then subtract every thought that has gone into any book that was taken from the Bible, and then search the laws of the nations and take out of every human government every truth that has been taken from the Bible, and then eliminate every name that has been copied from Scripture, and then take all the works of art, in painting, statuary or poetry, that have been copied from the Scriptures, and destroy them; and then go

into all the cemeteries in the world, and erase every text on every tomb that indicates the thought of a resurrection or immortality; and after we have subtracted every word, every Scripture, every thought, every trace of God's inspired Word from the world, it would be impossible for us to comprehend what the human race would be without a word of holy Scripture to guide it.

In a similar way, what would the history of the world be if there had been no prayer?

5. In all true prayer there remains something that is not answered in this present life, and there is a residue which remains to be answered in the great consummation when the saints are glorified, and when the history of redemption culminates in the judgment day.

In all true prayer there must be one continual thought and desire. Though it may not always be expressed in words, yet it is that which forms the essence of all prayer, which is the petition: "Thy kingdom come, thy will be done on earth, as it is in heaven." True prayer is divinely inspired, and God cannot inspire any prayer that does not look forward to the complete removal of sin from this earth, and the complete restoration of his kingdom and glory, and the doing of his will on earth as the angels do in heaven. Hence God must put his thought, and feeling, and purpose into every prayer which he inspires, although the one that is uttering the prayer may not grasp in detail all the things that God means by the prayer.

When we look out across the earth, we can see only a few miles of the earth's surface because it bends around in a circle, and our eye can grasp only a small arc of the circle. In a similar way, all things that come from God have a larger extension, beyond the grasp of our minds. And though our prayers may be answered, often times with remarkable precision, yet when they are answered in the most perfect degree, there still remains a fuller answer which is to come later on.

Now think of it: of the countless millions of prayers that have been offered in all generations, there is a residue to the answers to those prayers which will be manifest and fully answered in that great day when the glorified saints stand with their glorified High Priest, and have all their prayers presented to the Father for the last and perfect answer.

6. The depth and power and magnitude of our prayers depends on the spirit of sacrifice, consecration and obedience which is put into the prayer. This is revealed by the two altars that were in the tabernacle. The brazen altar was where the sacrifice was offered and burned, and the priest must always offer sacrifice first. Afterwards he went to the golden altar and offered the incense; and the effect of the incense and of the prayer, of which the incense was a type, was dependent on the work that had been accomplished in the sacrifice on the brazen altar.

The cross on which Christ died was his brazen altar, and after making that complete sacrifice, he then arose from the dead, and became the High Priest of intercession, and the power and efficiency of his intercession is based upon the merit of his sacrifice. Hence we read, in the passage under consideration, that he took fire from the altar with which to burn the incense before the throne.

The more perfectly we enter into the death of Jesus, the more powerful and prevailing will be our prayers.

7. Let us endeavor to comprehend what will be the answer which will come at last to all the prayers of God's people throughout all ages.

These prayers have been remembered by the Lord, though in so many instances forgotten by those who offered the prayer. These prayers not only sustain a relation to grace in rewards, but they also have a relation to the wicked, and administration of the judgments of God. You notice in the passage that when the High Priest set the prayers on fire, with fire taken from the altar, that those prayers were cast into the earth, and there were voices, and thunderings, and lightnings, and an earthquake, showing the connection between the prayers of the saints and the outpouring of the judgments of God on the wicked.

The altar was the basis upon which the prayers of the saints were offered, but that altar was rejected by the unbelieving world.

The blood of Christ was trampled on and treated as an unholy thing; the promises of God were ignored; the law of God was denied or denounced; and so in the winding up of the history of this world, every human being will be judged according to their attitude towards the altar where Christ shed his precious blood. Those who accept of that altar, and depend alone on the slain Lamb for their salvation, and to give efficiency to their prayers, will be lifted in fellowship with the great High Priest, to share his destiny and to enter into his joy: and on the other hand, those who rejected Christ, and despised his sacrifice, must be judged according to the righteousness expressed upon the altar of Christ's death.

God will measure everything in the human race according to the cross of Christ. Human beings go up or down according as they accept or reject of the slain Lamb. And hence, when the prayers of all saints are offered up before the eternal Father, the answer to those prayers will have a two-fold effect: an effect of glory for the righteous, and an effect of judgment for the wicked.

The snow falls on the tops of the Alps for many successive years, until the mountain tops are covered many feet thick with snow, and then, on some spring morning, the snow will begin to melt, and the weight is so great that it slips from the mountain top and forms an avalanche, rolling down the mountain side and crushing everything before it. This illustrates what is told in this Scripture, that when the prayers which the Saints of God have been sending up to the mountain of heaven, shall, in the judgment time, be let loose on the earth, there will be an awful desolation for those who have martyred the saints, persecuted the righteous, and robbed and defrauded the innocent and the helpless, and all the cries of the suffering righteous shall be answered in a perfect and adequate judgment upon those who have despised God and hated his righteous ones.

In the seventy-second Psalm, David offered a prayer for his son Solomon, but in reality it was for David's greater son, the Messiah; and in that psalm there is a picture of the millennium when Christ shall reign upon the earth, and the whole earth shall be filled with God's glory; and then follows a remarkable utterance: that the prayers of David, the son of Jesse, are ended. Many people misunderstand that verse, as to how David should stop praying.

The real meaning of the passage is, that when Christ reigns on the earth, and the world is full of God's glory, then all the prayers of David will have reached their ultimate fulfillment. Instead of its reading, "the prayers of David are ended," it should be *the prayers of David have reached their last perfect fulfillment.*

Now, in a similar way, our prayers will reach their last and perfect fulfillment in the glorified state, when Jesus reigns on the earth, and we can say that God's kingdom has come, and that his will is being done on earth as it is in heaven.

CHAPTER 11

The Eagles in Judgment

WHILE the great tribulation is taking place upon the nations on earth, a great many events of a different character will be taking place up in heaven with the glorified church. Among those things which will take place up in heaven will be the offering up of the prayers of all saints, and the assigning to the righteous their various rewards and places and ranks in the kingdom, and the singing of the great song of Moses and the Lamb, culminating in the marriage supper of the Lamb.

Another thing which is mentioned as taking place among the glorified saints, is that of participating with Christ in administering the judgments on the rebellious nations that are still alive on the earth. We are all familiar with the passage in 1 Cor. 6:2 and 3, that the saints are to judge the world, and to judge the angels, and with many it has been a question as to when that Scripture will be fulfilled. It is certain that the passage has not yet had its accomplishment, for at the present time the world judges the righteous; and oppresses and persecutes the servants of God; but during the great tribulation, the glorified saints who are with Christ up in heaven will begin their work in fellowship with Christ of judging the world.

This is referred to in Rev. 2:13: "And I beheld, and heard an eagle flying through the midst of heaven, saying with loud voice, Woe, woe, woe, to the inhabitants of the earth by reason of the other voices of the trumpet of the three angels, which are yet to sound!" In our Authorized Version it reads: "I heard an angel flying through heaven," but the word in the original is *eagle;* and the revised version has rendered it *one eagle.*

We have seen, in a previous chapter, that when the righteous dead were resurrected, and the living saints were translated and caught up through the door that was open in heaven, in Rev. 4: 1, that there were four living creatures in and about the throne having the faces of the lion, the calf, the man, and the eagle, which represent the highest rank among those who are saved from the earth. We have also seen, in Rev. 6, that when the Lamb began to open the seven seals, those four living creatures had authority to send forth the four horses, which we are told by Ezekiel, are the four sore judgments on the earth; and it was the office of the eagle to send forth the pale horse of death.

In all these passages we notice that the eagle saints will be called upon to take part with Jesus in sending forth the various calamities upon the ungodly nations, and to be participators with him in judging the world.

The word *judge* in the New Testament is used in two senses. In one sense the word means to discern, to understand or discriminate spiritual things, and this is the sense in which Saint Paul uses the word when he tells us that we ought to judge or discern ourselves, in order that we may not be judged. The other sense of the word is to affix rewards and penalties for conduct, rewarding the righteous and punishing the wicked; and in this sense of the word as we are commanded to judge no one until the time that the Lord shall come, when every man shall receive according to his works. Hence, in one sense we are to judge, that is, discern spiritual things in our present state of being; but in the sense of condemning people or punishing them, we are not to act as judges until in the judgment period when the world is punished for its sins. We see the double sense of the word *judge* in the life and kingdom of Jesus, for during his life on this earth he did not act as a judge in condemning people or punishing them, but he did judge all things in the sense of discerning, for he judged the hearts of all men and understood everything in the human race. But he will not act as a judge in the sense of condemning or rewarding people for their conduct until his second coming, and then he will judge the righteous for their rewards before his judgment seat, and judge the living nations on the earth for their wickedness, and especially the crime of rejecting him as the only Savior of the world.

In our further study upon this subject please notice the following points:

1. We are told that God the Father will judge no man, but that he has committed all judgment into the hands of the Son of man. By virtue of Christ's death and resurrection, he has achieved the honor and power to be the judge of all men in his humanity. Christ will not judge at the last day by virtue of his godhead or deity, but the Scriptures clearly show that he will act as judge as a man, and in the office of his humanity he will render the final decisions upon all men, whether good or bad, whether for rewards or punishments.

Now, inasmuch as Jesus is to be the judge in his humanity and as the Son of man, as we are told in the 5th chapter of Rev., he will take his glorified saints, the church of the firstborn, into fellowship with himself as co-regents and co-judges of the world. It is a great mistake for any Christian, during this present life, to attempt to sit on the judgment throne and condemn others, and assign various penalties to people, and whenever anyone undertakes that kind of thing they always fall from grace, and become subject to demoniac possession, and bring calamity and destruction upon themselves.

Like Jesus, we are to live in this life with meek and lowly hearts, discerning all things but not condemning them, patiently bearing all evil treatment and all trial, like Jesus did; and this longsuffering spirit in the love of God, forbearing with others, and enduring all things, is the very thing that will qualify the saints for taking part with Christ in the judgment day, and administering the penalties upon the ungodly world.

2. A sample of God's plan in taking the saints in union with Christ to judge the world is given in the formation of the kingdom of Israel. When God organized the twelve tribes of Israel into a kingdom at Mount Sinai, he arranged all the plan of their government under Moses as a pattern of things in the

heavenly kingdom. In the 24th chapter of Exodus we see that the Lord called Moses and Aaron, Nadab and Abihu, and seventy of the elders of Israel, up into Mount Sinai and revealed himself to them as sitting on the throne, on a sapphire pavement, and they ate and drank in the presence of God. Those seventy elders were formed into a national court to administer the affairs of the Hebrew kingdom. That court was perpetuated down to the time of Christ, and called the Sanhedrin, or the court of seventy elders. Jesus was tried before that court of seventy elders, and they condemned him to death.

Now, in a similar way, when the kingdom of heaven is fully set up at the second coming of Christ, we will see the twenty-four elders as described in Revelation, sitting on their throne around the throne of Christ, and acting in fellowship with Christ, and taking their part in judging the world, and administering all the affairs connected with the great tribulation.

God's plan for the Hebrews was that they should have no king except Jehovah, and that God would select, from time to time, elders from among the various tribes, and appoint them as judges of the people to act under the guidance of his Spirit, and in connection with instructions from inspired prophets that would be raised up. After awhile the Hebrew people insisted on having a king, and God acceded to their request, and under King David there was formed a pattern of the coming kingdom of heaven. But even then there were princes and elders who were to take part with the king in the administration of the government of the nation.

Nothing is more clearly told in the New Testament than the perfect oneness between Christ and his people, and this oneness is to be both in grace and in glory. Hence the apostle says, "If we suffer with him we shall also reign with him." If we share with Christ in this present life of humiliation, in faith and hope and love, we are also to share with him, in his second coming, in glory and royalty and in the functions of government.

3. It is in agreement with these remarks that we find the four living creatures and the twenty four elders, who represent the

bridehood saints in Revelation, sitting on thrones, and taking a very active part in all the results that follow the opening of the seven seals and the blowing of the seven trumpets.

The word "come" as used in Revelation 6, has been corrected in the revised version to *go*. When the first seal was opened, it was the living creature that had the face of a lion, and his voice was like thunder, and he said to the white horse, "Go." And then, when the second seal was opened, the second living creature that had the face of an ox, said "Go" to the red horse, and he went forth to scatter war and blood over the earth. And when the third seal was opened, it was the living creature with the face of a man that said "Go," to the black horse, to spread famine among the nations. And when he opened the fourth seal, it was the voice of the living creature that had the face of a flying eagle that said "Go," to the pale horse that spread death among the nations. Remember that these four living creatures represent a vast number of glorified saints in this rank, for it is said in another place, that they came from all nations and languages on the earth. Hence four is a typical number, and thus these living creatures exercised authority under the Lord Jesus to command the out-going of great judgments upon the earth. Under those four horses, we are told, one-fourth of the human beings on the earth were killed with the sword and hunger and death and wild beasts of the earth. According to Scripture, at the time of the great tribulation, under the out-going of the four horses, there will be slain one-fourth of the human race, amounting to at least four hundred million human beings, compared to which all the wars we have ever read about are a drop in the bucket.

These glorified saints who will thus take part with Jesus in judging the world, will be those who in their lifetime on earth were persecuted and slain, misjudged, and who suffered every indignity at the hands of ungodly men, and bore all their suffer-ings with a meek and patient spirit, praying for their enemies. But when at last the judgment is set in, the great God will take these heroic saints and set them on thrones, in fellowship with the enthroned Son of man, and have them take part with Jesus in administering the awful penalties coming upon this world.

It is in harmony with these remarks that we see this eagle sent forth, in chapter 8, to cry, with a loud voice, "Woe to the inhabitants of the earth," and warning them of the still greater calamities that are coming upon them.

In examining those passages in Scripture where the saints are to take part with Christ in administering the great tribulation judgment, we must remember that it will be in fulfillment of many prophecies in the Old Testament.

Many have been puzzled to know what it means in Psalm 149, where we read: "Let the saints be joyful in glory," (that is, in the glorified state); "and let the high praises of God be in their mouth, and a two-edged sword in their hand: to execute vengeance upon the heathen" (or the nations), "and punishments upon the people: to bind their kings with chains, and their nobles with fetters of iron; to execute upon them" (the wicked) "the judgment written: this honor have all his saints."

This prophecy is one among many that will be literally fulfilled in the great tribulation when the eagle saints, the living creatures, and the glorified elders, will exercise authority under the Lord Jesus to administer the penalties upon the wicked world.

Another instance of the saints' judging the world is referred to in Rev. 11, where the apostle had a reed like a rod given to him, and he was commanded to rise and measure the temple of God, and the altar, and them that worship therein. That Scripture evidently refers to the restoration of Israel, and the rebuilding of the temple, which will take place probably during the great tribulation, and is always spoken of as an event that will occur in the time of judgment. The prophet speaks of Israel being restored in judgment. And in this time of the restoration of Israel, it would seem that the glorified saints are to take part with Christ as ministering angels to gather out the people of Israel from all of the nations on the earth, and lead them to their own land.

If you do not believe these things that I am writing about, what will you do with the words of Jesus in Matthew 19:27-30?

Peter was asking the Lord as to what rewards the apostles should receive for leaving all and following Christ. Jesus said to them: "Verily I say unto you, That ye which have followed me in the regeneration" (that is, in the restoration) "when the Son of man shall sit in the throne of his glory, ye also shall sit upon twelve thrones, judging the twelve tribes of Israel." Unless we take these words literally, to mean just exactly what they say, then they mean nothing at all. The people that undertake to spiritualize these words, and say it means nothing more than that those who follow Christ are to have a good influence over the people, simply render the Word of God without effect, and turn the words of God into nonsense. Mark you, these words, it is distinctly affirmed, will never be accomplished until the second coming of Christ, when he, the Son of Man, shall sit in the throne of his glory; and so it cannot refer to the power of Christian influence in the present life, for it will take place only at the judgment time when Christ will come again. Here we see that the glorified saints are to deal with the restoration of Israel, and take part not only in administering the wrath of God on the ungodly nations, but also take part with Christ in governing the twelve tribes of Israel after they are restored to their own land, and have accepted the Lord Jesus as their Messiah.

Another instance in which the eagle saints are to judge the world is found in Rev. 20:4: "And I saw thrones, and they sat upon them, and judgment" (that is, power to judge) "was given unto them; and I saw the souls of them that were beheaded for the witness of Jesus, and for the word of God; and they lived and reigned with Christ a thousand years." Remember, the thousand-year reign is included in the great day of judgment which will last a thousand years, and that it is in that time that the glorified saints shall judge the nations who are still living on the earth, and administer all the affairs of the Messianic government upon the people that will be born and live in that age. When the glorified saints judge the nations in the thousand-year reign, it does not mean that they will punish those nations, but that they will act as judges, similar to what Samuel did in ancient Israel, and that all the affairs of the nations on the earth will be put under the infallible guidance and wisdom and authority of the glorified saints.

This is what Isaiah prophesies when he says: "Behold, a king shall reign in righteousness, and princes shall rule in judgment. And a man shall be as an hiding place from the wind, and a covert from the tempest: as rivers of waters in a dry place, as the shadow of a great rock in a weary land" (Isa. 32:1-2).

That king is Jesus, and those princes are the glorified saints: and while Jesus will be absolute king over all, yet under him and united to him will be these princes, the eagle saints, who will act under his direction in administering all the affairs of the human race. And those glorified saints will be the protectors of the nations – as the prophet says, as an hiding place from the wind, and as a covert from the tempest, and out of their inner being will flow rivers of water in dry places, and they will serve as the shadow of a great rock in a weary land. And then the prophet goes on to show that under their righteous administration among the nations, the heart of the rash shall understand knowledge, and the tongue of the stammerers shall speak plainly, and a vile person shall no longer be praised, nor a churl said to be bountiful. And the characters of all men will be properly judged, and there will be no fraud or deception, and no partiality allowed among men.

In concluding this chapter, let us remember that there are certain qualifications which are essential to rulership and to being a judge. Humility of spirit is the greatest essential in being a ruler over mankind. It is said that Moses was the meekest man on the earth, and hence God selected him to be the great ruler and leader of Israel. Jesus was preeminently the most humble man that ever lived in the world, and as a man his boundless humility and meekness of spirit qualify him to be the judge of all men and the ruler of the world. Just as Moses, and Samuel, and David, and other great judges in ancient Israel were called and appointed by the Lord alone, and they were at an infinite distance from appointing themselves, so it will be in the coming kingdom, for God himself will select and appoint all saints to their ranks and their spheres of office, and give to each one his duty and his authority.

Just as the crucified Jesus is the one who is to judge the world, in the same body in which he was crucified, so those saints who take part with Christ in judging the world are those who have been crucified with Christ, and have been baptized into his suffering, and shared in the depth of his humility and boundless charity.

The throne will be the outcome of the cross, and those who share the cross will share the throne; and those who rejected the cross will have no throne. There will be a perfect correspondence between the services of the glorified saints and their life and labor in this present world. It is in the light of all these considerations and Scriptures that we are to understand what it will mean when the saints shall judge the world, and fulfill, in the great judgment period, God's plans which will be the proper outcome of what is now being wrought out in the experiences of grace, in the present state of probation.

CHAPTER 12

The Judgment and Reward of the Saints

AS we follow in Scripture the successive steps in the destiny of the saints, we find that after the righteous dead are resurrected, and the living saints are translated to meet Christ in the air, the next thing is that they stand before the judgment seat of Christ, and each one gives an account of himself according to the deeds done in the body, and they are judged for their rewards, and receive their crowns, and their positions and rank in the kingdom of God.

It is difficult to get Christian people to understand the teaching of Scripture about the second coming of Christ and the judgment day, because for hundreds of years the theology of the church on these subjects has been taken from the poets, such as Dante and Milton and Pollock, instead of from the Scriptures. The Bible sets forth a regular series of successive events in the judgment day, just as orderly and precise as were the steps in the six days of creation at the beginning of the world. God works with a distinct method, and not in confusion, and the world will have its winding up just as orderly as it had its beginning.

According to Scripture, the judgment day will last a thousand years. Peter tells us that there is to be a day of judgment, and in the very next verse he tells us that that day will be a thousand years (2 Peter 3:7-8). All the 140 Scriptures on the judgment day reveal the fact that the saints are judged first, then the apostate church is judged next; and then the wicked world, or the nations living in the flesh, are judged next, and then Satan and the wicked dead are judged last. Peter tells us that judgment must begin at the house of God. In all the parables on the judgment, Jesus teaches us that the best saints will be judged first; for instance,

121

the man who had ten pounds was judged first, and then the man with five pounds, and then the man with one, and the wicked nations that would not accept of him were judged last.

In the fiftieth Psalm there is a perfect setting forth of the second coming of Christ and the judgment, and we see there that "our God shall come, and he shall call to the heavens and the earth, and gather his saints unto himself; those who have made a covenant with him"; and then follows the judgment on the ungodly church that simply offered him an outward worship in sacrifices and material things, but did not give him the love of their hearts. And then, from verse 16, follows the judgment of the ungodly nations for all of their crimes, and they are to have their sins set before their eyes, and be torn to pieces.

In the Book of Revelation we see the saints are called up through the open door in the beginning of chapter 4, and in a short while after that, we see the living creatures, which are redeemed men, and the elders there, with golden crowns, seated on their thrones, showing that they have passed their judgment and received their crowns. Then follows, in chapter 5, the great tribulation judgment, which runs on to chapter 19, when the Antichrist is destroyed. Then follows the thousand years' reign, which is really included in the judgment day, for it is during that period that the saints are to judge the world; that is, be rulers over the earth, and have power to judge committed to them. And after the thousand years' reign, the great white throne is set up, and Satan is judged, and the wicked dead are raised and judged for their sins and receive their doom, which closes the judgment day.

Hence the judgment day includes three distinct aspects of judgment. First, that of the saints, and then that of the living nations on the earth, and then that of the wicked dead. We now want to study especially the judgment of the saints, and the apostle tells us that the saints are not to be judged with the world, and hence it forms a distinct chapter in the winding up of human history. The Scripture that especially presents that subject to us is found in 1 Cor. 3:11-15. "For other foundation can no man lay than that is laid, which is Jesus Christ. Now if any man build upon this foundation gold, silver, precious stones, wood, hay, stubble; every man's work shall be made manifest: for the day shall declare it; because it shall be revealed by fire; and the fire shall try every man's work of what sort it is. If any man's work abide" (or pass through the fire test) "which he hath built there-upon, he shall receive a reward. If any man's work shall be burned, he shall suffer loss: but he himself shall be saved; yet so as by fire."

This is perhaps the most remarkable passage in the entire Bible, in setting forth the nature and different degrees of judg-ment pertaining to the righteous. There are words in this passage which nobody on earth could ever imagine how they would be accomplished until in the light of modern science they have been so illuminated as to become perfectly transparent.

1. The foundation of all Christian faith and practice is that of Jesus Christ. "Other foundation can no man lay than that is laid, which is Jesus Christ." This foundation is the basis of all saving faith, and also the basis of all good works that are wrought in Christ by the Spirit, and the meaning of the word is: There is no other person or religion in the whole world, or throughout all ages, by which anyone can be saved or by which good works can be wrought that are acceptable to God, except through Jesus Christ.

We must here distinguish between saving faith and rewards, for so many professing Christians are in the dark concerning the difference between salvation and rewards. We are saved by faith in Christ alone, without any merit of our works; but we are reward-ed according to our works, the deeds we do in the body before death. Saving faith is instantaneous, but good works are gradual and accumulative. Saving faith is depending on Christ alone to forgive us and cleanse us; but good works are to be wrought out from our saving faith according to our ability and knowledge and zeal. Saving faith admits us into the heavenly kingdom, but rewards for good works will decide our station and rank in the kingdom, and our degree of glory and usefulness in the ages to come. Saving faith is for this present life, but rewards are given to us only at the second coming of Christ and at the judgment seat of Christ. We are justified by faith, and walk by faith, and overcome the world by faith; but, according to Scripture, no one gets his final reward until at the resurrection of the righteous, or the translation of the saints. We are all saved alike, but we are all rewarded in different degrees according to our works.

People often say of a good man that he has died and gone to his reward; but such a remark is contrary to the Word of God, for every Scripture bearing on the subject speaks of the righteous dead, that "they have entered into rest," that "they have gone to paradise," that they are "taken to be with the Lord," and "their works do follow them," and they are awaiting the second coming of Christ to get their glorified bodies. On the other hand, every Scripture, in referring to the subject, teaches that no rewards are given until Jesus comes the second time. And Christ says: "I come quickly, and my reward is with me, to give every one according to his works."

2. Let us notice the different materials that Christian people build with upon the foundation. All who trust in Christ alone to save them are standing on the true foundation. But there is a great difference in the lives of Christian people, and in the kinds of material that they build with, and in the character of their works and of their rewards. The apostle mentions six things which represent the different building materials, viz.: gold, silver, precious stones – which are non-combustible; and then wood, hay and stubble, which are combustible.

There are several passages in the New Testament which refer to the two classes of believers who are designated as carnal and spiritual. The apostle Paul speaks of the class of Christians that he calls babes in Christ, who are yet carnal, and governed largely by their natural feelings and opinions. He speaks of others as "being spiritual," as "being perfect," as being "able to discern all things," and these are those who are governed by the Holy Spirit, who have pure motives and pure intentions, and who live according to the power of Christ ruling in them.

There are two words whereby the apostle refers to these two classes: one is the word "soulish," translated *natural,* and the other is the word "spiritual." Multitudes of Christians are religious in their souls or natural feelings and sentiments, but they are not spiritual, and do not see or act according to the Holy Ghost. There are other Christians who have been purified from the carnal mind, and received the indwelling of the Holy Spirit, and who work in the spirit and not in the flesh.

It is very evident that every Christian will build his religious life according to the degree of the saving grace he has, and according to the power of his motives and intentions, whether they are carnal or spiritual, or whether they be mixed.

In tropical cities, we often see big stone houses most substantially built, and on the very next lot there may be a house built of bamboo or of wood with a grass roof. If a fire breaks out, of course the grass house burns immediately, but the thick stone walls of the other building resist the flames.

This is the illustration that Paul uses in the passage. All the houses are built on the same foundation, but of such diverse materials as to take an infinite difference in case of conflagration.

You will notice in this passage which I am expounding that although Christian believers are building on Christ, the true Foundation, yet the materials of their building are of a mixed character, partly carnal and partly spiritual in many cases, and this mixedness enters into every part of Christian life and service, and it will never be known until in the judgment, which things are of gold and silver and precious stones, and which things are of wood, hay and stubble. For instance, Christian ministers who are not thoroughly purified and illuminated by the Holy Spirit, will put into their sermons truth and error, Christ and self, the things of the spirit and the things of the flesh, seeking in some measure to glorify Christ, and at the same time in many ways seeking to glorify self, and to advance their own material honor and reputation and self-interest; oftentimes preaching in one sermon what they contradict in another, because the mixedness of their religious experience will of necessity be imparted to their preaching. Also, in the prayers which Christians present to God, there is in most cases much of selfishness in multiplied forms, mixed in with what is true scriptural praying; and many prayers are loaded down with so much of self that they cannot rise to heaven. Also in religious teaching, in books and Bible lectures, there is so much mixedness of truth and error, of the perverting of the Word of God, of allowing one's religious creed or denominational theology to override the true interpretation of God's Word. Also in our religious motives there may be much which is intended to please God, yet multitudes of Christians have motives of self-seeking in their religion, in the building of churches and religious institutions, in the carrying on of missionary enterprises, in the training of children; and in everything that pertains to the Christian life, there is so much carnality and selfish sectarianism mingled in with true Christian faith.

Now God is the only one that is liable to look through this great mass of religious life and the building of Christian character and work, and discern how much is of the spirit and how much is of the flesh. And when the believer stands before the judgment seat of Christ, there will then take place the sifting of the true from the false, and of self from Christ, and a complete separation of those elements which partake of gold, silver and precious stones, and those other elements which partake of wood, hay and stubble.

3. Let us now examine the third statement in the passage. that "every man's work shall be made manifest, for the day shall declare it, because it shall be revealed by fire, and the fire shall try every man's work, of what sort it is." It would seem from these words that the life-work of every servant of God will not be clearly and openly manifested until this judgment of the saints comes to pass. Although countless millions of believers have died, and their spirits are now resting in paradise, yet their life-work has not yet been judged, and the various principles in their character and work have not yet been manifested, either to themselves or to the heavenly world.

It is impossible for anyone of us in this life to understand all the details of our actions, because of the mixed condition of things in our lives, and because of the infirmity of our minds in the present state. No action can ever be seen in the present life in its fullness, for in the nature of things there is always an unseen moral and spiritual quality in every act which can never be made known in this life. When icebergs are seen floating in the ocean, we are told that seven-tenths of the iceberg is in the water and only three-tenths of it is visible to the eye, and this may serve to illustrate the nature of all our actions and our conduct and words; for, while a certain part of every act can be known and judged of in a measure, yet the greater part of our actions and words is submerged, as it were, in a spiritual sea, and we never can fathom or measure all the parts or ascertain the magnitude of any action or any word. The same act may be performed by a hundred different persons, and yet the act may contain as many different forms and degrees of character, so that the same act would not receive the same degree of reward or of punishment to each person, because of the unknown quality that is put into the act by each person.

The discovery of the X-ray gives us a perfect illustration of the way our actions and lives will be manifested at the judgment seat of Christ. We are told in this passage that the fire will make manifest every man's work, of what sort it is, and for thousands of years no one on earth has ever been able to imagine how fire could reveal a man's actions and find the true quality of those actions. Some years ago my wife and myself were in the office of a physician who had an X-ray apparatus, and he shut off all the light in the room and turned on the X-ray machine; my wife stood and held out her arm, and the light from the electric machine passed through an inch plank, and a lot of paper, and the clothing on my wife's arm and her flesh, and when I looked I saw only the bones in her arm! If someone had prophesied fifty years ago that the bones in a person's body could be manifested by fire, it would have been impossible for the whole human race to have imagined how the thing could be done without burning the flesh. But now, behold! This marvelous instrument of electricity can reveal every part of the human body without burning a single atom of it. In the same way, God has some method, at present unknown to us, by which a divine fire can be turned onto every man's life work and reveal just exactly the moral and spiritual qualities of the life work and make manifest to the intelligence of all the saints and the universe what is the quality of every act and every word and every thought that is expressed by a human being.

When Hannah, the mother of Samuel, visited Shiloh the second time, and presented her little boy to the Lord, she received the anointing of the Holy Spirit, and under that baptism uttered a wonderful prophecy in which she said that Jehovah was a God of knowledge, and that by him actions were weighed. That is a wonderful expression – that God should weigh our actions and our words and our thoughts and be able to manifest to others the exact specific gravity of all actions and of all conduct.

The government in Washington has a pair of scales so delicate that you can put a piece of thin paper in the scales and weigh it, and then write with a lead pencil on that same piece of paper and weigh it again, and the scales will reveal not only the weight of the paper but also the weight of the amount of lead that was put on the paper from the pencil. This is a faint illustration of the way in which God will manifest in the judgment time the character and color and weight and dimension of all the actions and words, and even the thoughts of his people.

This judgment of the saints must of necessity take place in order that each one may receive his proper reward and his rank in the kingdom of God, and also it must take place before the marriage of the Lamb with his elect saints.

4. Let us, in the next place, look at the subject of loss and rewards that will come to the Lord's people as a result of this final judgment. "If any man's work abide the fire test, which he hath built thereupon, he shall receive a reward; but if any man's work shall be burned, he shall suffer loss, but he himself shall be saved; yet so as by fire." This passage proves positively that great multitudes will be saved who will yet suffer loss because their works have not been according to the truth of Scripture, or have not been wrought in the love of God, and will be burned.

We must remember that salvation is one thing and rewards is quite another. What a vast conflagration will take place at that judgment seat when such a vast amount of erroneous sermons and false books and selfish prayers and selfish giving of money and carnal religious work will be burned up because they partake of the nature of wood, hay and stubble! Many a fine sermon, many a beautiful song, many an eloquent prayer, and millions of money that have been given for selfish motives and sectarian pride, and so much busy service wrought in the flesh, will be utterly destroyed and get no reward because it will not be able to stand the X-ray test of the judgment. The apostle John urges believers to so work that they will not be ashamed to meet the Lord, implying that some will meet him and be ashamed.

The Bible supplies us with examples of everything in the world, and in the cases of Abraham and Lot we have specimens of the two kinds of religious work. Abraham walked before God and was perfect, and his work will stand the fire test. But, on the other hand, Lot, although he is called a righteous man – that is, a justified man – yet pitched his tent towards Sodom, and every bit of his property was burned in the fire, and the angel had to pull him out of the fire to save his life, which agrees exactly with the apostle's words, that their works were burned up, yet they were saved, so as by fire. The life-work of Lot was of wood, hay and stubble and was burned; but the life-work of Abraham was of gold, silver and precious stones, which are non-combustible and which endured the final test.

There will be no reward given for the life-work of any believer except for those things that shall escape the fire, for the apostle says, "If any man's work abide" – that is, pass the fire test – "he shall receive a reward."

There is a vast world of truth opened to our study in connection with the rewards which the saved ones will receive for their good works. In the first place, the reward will correspond exactly to the quality of the action, and also to the magnitude or the weight of the action, and also to the amount of divine love or of sacrifice or of faith or of perseverance that has been put into action, so that the reward will fit the act as perfectly as the skin fits the flesh. These rewards will extend down to the littlest things in our life as well as to the greatest, for the prophet Malachi tells us that God will reward his people for even thinking upon his name, and Jesus tells us that there will be a reward given to those who give a cup of cold water to another in the name of the Lord Jesus; from which we learn that the system of Divine rewards will correspond to the system of nature, which is just as perfect in the formation of the eye or the wing of a house fly as it is in the formation of the vast system of suns and stars.

The consideration of these things should certainly inspire us to the utmost devotion and the putting into our life-work of as much of Christ and his truth as we possibly can.

We find a good illustration upon this subject in the life of the apostle Paul, for the first part of his life was intensely Jewish and sectarian and selfish and filled with the carnal mind; and when he became a Christian he said that he suffered the loss of all things; that is, all honor and fame and power which he had acquired by his zeal for Judaism was burned up. But the life he lived as a Christian was built of gold, silver and precious stones, and for that life he will receive a great reward at the coming of the Lord. So the first part of his life, although it was intensely religious, was also wood, hay and stubble, but his Christian life was built of precious gems which the fire cannot burn.

5. There is another subject, that is not mentioned in this passage but that is referred to in another Scripture, which will be settled at the judgment seat of Christ, and that is, that all the misunderstandings and disagreements of God's people throughout all generations will have to be clarified and settled up in the presence of the Lord Jesus at the judgment of the saints. Only think of all the disagreements and misunderstandings and earthly prejudices which have existed among God's people in all generations – as between Jew and Gentile, as between Calvinist and Arminian, as between High and Low Church, and all the misunderstandings between individuals! In fact, everything that has interfered in this life with the fellowship and the mutual love of all God's people will have to be explained and settled in the clear light of God before the judgment seat. It is utterly absurd to

suppose that all God's people can go on living throughout ever-lasting ages in the kingdom of God, and carry along with them all the foolish disagreements and all the prejudices that existed in them up to the point of their death. There must be a perfect, divine adjustment of every believer, not only in harmony with Christ, but in harmony with all others, so that not one single soul in the heavenly kingdom will be in disagreement with any other soul. This is what Paul teaches when he says that Jesus Christ will reconcile all things to himself, not only which are on earth but also which are in heaven. A beautiful illustration as well as a prophetic sample of this is found in the life of Job, that after he passed through his severe trials, his three friends, who were all of them prophets or preachers, and who had misunderstood Job and misjudged him, had to make a second visit to Job and get perfectly adjusted to him, in mutual reconciliation and love and respect, and they had to offer sacrifice and have Job pray for them that they might be brought into perfect unity of heart and mind. And you may depend on it, that is a sample of what will take place in the case of God's servants who have lived and died and have gone into paradise: but they will have to get harmonized with each other in the heavenly kingdom right in the presence of the blessed Jesus, who is not only the Savior of his people, but the Judge also.

Countless thousands of believers who will be saved in heaven have criticized the bridehood saints and persecuted those who were sanctified. But at the judgment day, in the presence of Jesus, they will change their tune and will praise and honor the very saints that in this life they criticized and spurned. This is referred to in Scripture where it speaks of the daughters – that is, the companies of saved ones – when they see the illustrious beauty and glory of the bridehood saints, they will praise her and give due honor to those who in this life were most devoted to the Lord Jesus.

Nothing will pass the judgment seat of Christ except that which is perfect truth and perfect love and such things as are fit to endure throughout everlasting ages – the light and truth of God.

CHAPTER 13

The Song of Moses and the Lamb

AS I have remarked in another place, during the great tribulation judgment upon the earth there will be many things that will take place with the glorified church, with Christ up in heaven. It is during that time that Christ, as the great High Priest, will gather up the prayers of all the saints that have ever lived on the earth, and present them to the Father with much incense, and the effect of those prayers will result in the consummation of the judgments on those who have rejected the great sacrifice of Christ for the sins of the world.

Another event of a similar character will be the singing of the song of Moses and the song of the Lamb, which is recorded in Rev. 15:1-4. The prayers of all saints has a special reference to the office of priests, which includes the offering of sacrifice, and kindling the fire on the altar, and swinging the censer of intercessory prayer. On the other hand, the singing of the great song of Moses and the Lamb belongs to the prophetic office, and includes playing on harps, and singing both psalms and hymns, and the utterance of inspired poetry and testimony. These are the thoughts which are expressed in the passage that we want to analyze.

"And I saw another sign in heaven, great and marvelous, seven angels having the seven last plagues, for in them is filled up the wrath of God. And I saw as it were a sea of glass mingled with fire; and them that had gotten the victory over the beast, and over his mark, and over the number of his name, stand on the sea of glass, having the harps of God. And they sing the song of Moses the servant of God, and the song of the Lamb, saying, Great and marvelous are thy works, Lord God Almighty; just and true are thy ways, thou King of saints. Who shall not fear thee, O Lord, and glorify thy name? for thou only art holy: for all nations shall come and worship before thee; for thy judgments are made manifest" (Rev. 15 :1-4).

The first thing to observe in this passage is the *glassy sea*. To get an understanding of this we must go back and find where it is first referred to in the Scriptures. When the Hebrews crossed the Red Sea, they were delivered from their bondage and from the tyranny of Pharaoh, who was a type of the Antichrist or the great beast that is to arise in the tribulation judgment. After reaching the eastern shore of the Red Sea, when the waters returned and drowned the Egyptians, Miriam and a company of women joined with her, took their timbrels and marched up and down on the seashore, praising God for their deliverance, while the waters of the Red Sea stretched out before them like a glassy mirror gleaming in the morning sun.

"Then sang Moses and the children of Israel this song unto the Lord, saying, I will sing unto the Lord, for he hath triumphed gloriously: the horse and his rider hath he thrown into the sea. The Lord is my strength and song, and he is become my salvation: he is my God, and I will prepare him an habitation; my father's God, and I will exalt him. Pharaoh's chariots and his host hath he cast into the sea: his chosen captains also are drowned in the Red Sea. And Miriam the prophetess, the sister of Aaron, took a timbrel in her hand; and all the women went out after her with timbrels and with dances, and they said: Sing ye to the Lord, for he hath triumphed gloriously" (Exod. 15:1-20).

They had gotten the victory over the great beast of Egyptian tyranny, and over all the slave marks which had been put upon them, and with their timbrels they sang the song of triumph.

The next time we find reference to the glassy sea is when Moses and Aaron, Nadab, and Abihu, and seventy of the elders went up into Mount Sinai, and they saw the God of Israel, and there was under his feet as it were a paved work of a sapphire stone, and as it were the body of heaven in his clearness. And upon the nobles of the children of Israel he laid not his hand:

also they saw God and did eat and drink" (Ex. 24:9-11). This was a most remarkable prophetic event, setting forth in type the time when the church of the firstborn – the living creatures and the elders – should be called up into heaven and stand on the glassy sea, having the harps of God.

The next time we see any reference to the glassy sea is in the building of the temple by Solomon. "And he made a molten sea, ten cubits from the one brim to the other" (which is fifteen feet) "it was round all about, and his height was five cubits: and a line of thirty cubits did compass it round about" (1 Kings 7:23). This molten sea was in the temple before the throne, and was a prophetic image of what we have in Revelation 15.

The next reference to the glassy sea is in Revelation 4:6, where the living creatures and the elders, which represent the church of the firstborn – the true eagle saints – were caught up through the open door into heaven, and were seen in relation to the throne and to a sea of glass like unto crystal.

There is a perfect agreement among all these portions of Scripture, proving a perfect unity as to the locality and the use of this glassy sea. It is up in the sky; it is before the throne of God, and it is a place where the translated and glorified saints assemble to praise God for their deliverance from everything connected with the beast or the Antichrist.

The next item to be studied is that of their having the harps of God, which, as I have said, proves the office work of prophets. When Samuel anointed Saul to be king of Israel, he told Saul that he would meet a company of prophets playing on their harps and prophesying. At another time, a prophet called for a harp to be played that he might, under its inspiration, give forth the word of the Lord. King David speaks of uttering prophetic sentences with a harp. Isaiah draws a picture of the victorious saints of God, playing on their harps in connection with the judgments of God on the Antichrist.

"Behold, the Lord cometh with burning and anger and full of indignation. And ye saints shall have a song, and gladness of heart, as when one goeth with a pipe to come into the mountain of the Lord. And the Lord shall cause his voice to be heard, and shall show the lighting down of his arm with indignation, like a tempest and hailstones. And when the Lord shall lay on the enemy his staff, it shall be with tabrets and harps. For Tophet is ordained of old, for the king" (that is, the Antichrist) (Isaiah 30:27-33).

This prophetic passage from Isaiah is in perfect agreement with the passage from Revelation 15, that when the Antichrist, the great beast, is overthrown, the victorious and glorified servants of God will rejoice and express their gladness and praises by playing on the harps of God. But the main thing in this passage which we want to study is the song of Moses and the song of the Lamb.

The song of Moses celebrates the works of the Lord in creation. "Great and marvelous are thy works, Lord God Almighty." The song of the Lamb celebrates the ways of God in his thoughts and plans with regard to redemption.

The song of Moses refers to the external universe, the wonders and mysteries that are expressed in the material creation. The song of the Lamb sets forth the inward life of God, the perfections of his moral character and the hidden glories of his love and grace in forming a plan to save sinners, which can never he known except by a revelation through his own Son who lives in the bosom of the Father.

1. Let us, in the first place, study the song of Moses, the servant of God, which celebrates the magnitude and the marvelous wonders of the works of God in creation. We must remember that Moses writes out the account of creation as God revealed it to him in a vision, as to the origin and the successive steps in forming the world.

There are some who teach that Moses wrote the account of creation only as he had it from the lips of tradition, as it was handed down from Adam through the patriarchs. It is true that the early fathers of the human race did transmit verbal accounts of God's dealings with them and with the world: but Adam did not see the creation when it was formed, and it makes the Word of God a very slender thing to have it depend only on tradition. God gave Moses a look or a vision backward, and he caused the successive scenes of creation to pass before his eyes, so that he wrote the account under the direct and infallible inspiration of the Holy Spirit, and as he saw the successive periods go by, in a kind of moving picture.

The book of Revelation was given to St. John in the Isle of Patmos in a similar way. John was allowed to have a forward look into the second coming of Christ, and he saw pass in review before his eyes the successive steps in connection with the church age, which concludes with the third chapter; and then the open door, in chapter four, and the catching up of the church of the firstborn – the living creatures and the elders – and then the opening of the seven seals, and the successive steps in the great tribulation judgment, down to the destruction of the Antichrist, the chaining of Satan, and the thousand-year reign of the saints on earth, and onward into the new creation and the city of the New Jerusalem.

And just as John had a forward look into events connected with the winding up of the history of this world, so Moses had a backward look as to the successive periods in the origin of the world, and the formation of all things material or animal or human. Hence it is perfectly appropriate to designate the song of the works of God as being the song of Moses – that chosen servant who saw and recorded the creation of the material universe.

Now there are two words which characterize this song of Moses: the word "great" and the word "marvelous." The word "great" refers to the inconceivable magnitudes of creation, and the word "marvelous" refers to the infinitesimal of all things in the creation. The greatness of creation is spread out before us through the instrument of the telescope, and the marvelous wonders of creation are revealed to us, through the instrument of the microscope.

Let us notice the greatness of the works of God. By the use of the telescope the greatness of the material universe has been brought to our knowledge in such a degree as to be beyond the power of all imagination to even grasp a small fraction of the works of God. It looks to us as if the world on which we live is a very large thing, and yet when we come to study the magnitudes of creation, our earth is only a small grain of sand on the shores of the universe. The sun of our solar system is so large that, if it were hollow, this globe could be put in the center of it, and our moon sustain the same relation to it that it does now, revolving about the earth, and this world would be to the sun like a garden pea in the center of an empty flour barrel, or rather like the head of a pin in the center of a great hogshead; for the sun is millions of times larger than our earth. And then the North Star is fifty times larger than our sun, but so far away that the distance cannot be measured by miles, but only by the speed of light. Light travels about a hundred thousand miles a second. The light from the sun, which is ninety-three million miles away, reaches our earth in about eight minutes. But the North Star is so very far away that it has been estimated that it takes over forty years for the light to come from the North Star to our earth.

That great North Star travels around the Seven Stars, and they in turn travel around some great unknown center in space, which may be, so far as we know, the throne of God.

It has been estimated by astronomers that our solar system is traveling around other larger systems, and that it requires about eighteen million years for these systems to make one complete revolution around the universe. This seems to agree with what David says in the 19th Psalm: that our sun is like a bridegroom coming out of his chamber, and a strong man to run a race, and that his going forth is from one end of heaven, and his circuit unto the ends of it; which seems to imply that our solar system does indeed revolve around the universe from one end of creation to the other end of it. This gives us the magnitude of the works of God, absolutely inconceivable to any human mind.

Suppose a man driving an automobile at the rate of twenty miles an hour should have an accident by which one spoke of one wheel should he broken, and suppose that the man was so powerful and so skillful that he could repair the broken spoke without stopping the machine, and do it before the wheel had made one ten-thousandth part of a revolution. We would regard it as a feat of supernatural skill. We may regard this earth as a little spoke in the vast wheel of creation, and we may regard the fall of Adam as a break in that spoke, and yet if we count the time from the fall of Adam to the time of the new creation when all things will be restored to their original glory, the time taken of the seven thousand years would be accomplished before our solar system had made one ten-thousandth part of a revolution around the center of the universe.

It is evident that the glorified saints will have the ability to search into and become acquainted with the vastness of all the works of God.

The other word is "marvelous," which introduces us to the minute things of creation, as brought to our knowledge by the microscope. Dr. Young, in his "Night Thoughts," has represented that God made man just midway between the infinitely small and the infinitely great in his universe. This poetical thought, so far as we know, may be true, and if so, then there is a universe that lies beneath us in the infinitesimal, as marvelous as is the creation above us. The microscope has discovered many features in the common house fly, in the structure of its body and the number of its eyes and the various movements it has, which are just as wonderful as the stellar universe. A drop of water from a mud hole, under the strongest microscope, will bring to view whole armies of living creatures too small for the unaided eye to see. All those minute creatures are born, and live, and die, like larger animals, and have their wars and marchings, and modes of happiness, on a scale so small as to be beyond the comprehension of the human mind. In every leaf, and every blade of grass, and every grain of sand, and every drop of blood, there are whole worlds of wonders – distinct species of creatures, with peculiar modes of life and motion, which reveal the fact that the great Creator is absolutely infinite, and reveals his skill and power in things beneath our notice as completely as in those great worlds that float above us in distant space.

When we consider all these facts, and then remember that this God is our God, that he numbers the hairs upon our heads and knows the drops of blood in our veins, and estimates every minute thing in our souls and bodies, and knows every thought in our minds, and every emotion in our hearts, it should certainly impress us with a disposition of complete and boundless confidence in such a God; for how true it is that in him we live and move and have our being. We shall never he able to appreciate these facts with regard to the creation until we are lifted into a glorified state.

2. In the second place, let us consider the song of the Lamb. "Just and true are thy ways, thou King of Saints."

In this connection I want to call your attention to a thought that I have never seen in print in any book outside of the Bible, and to which I have never in my life heard anyone refer, and the thought is, that Jesus Christ, the Lamb of God, is an infinite musician, and sings a song that is infinite in every perfection connected with song or singing. Have you ever thought it over, that Jesus is a singer, and that he will take part in leading this great song of Moses and the Lamb? We often hear of David sweeping his harp and singing his sweet psalms, but why should we overlook the fact that the Lord will have his harp, and be the choir leader in that ultimate song of complete victory which will be sung on the glassy sea?

After Jesus finished the Last Supper, and was on his way with the eleven disciples to the Garden of Gethsemane, to enter into the most awful sufferings that have ever been in the world – while on that journey from the Last Supper to the agony in the garden, and to the cross – we are told that they sang a psalm. Only think of it! Jesus was going into the storm of unutterable anguish, and yet he went with a song on his lips, repeating in melodious measures one of the psalms that were sung by the priests at the time of the passover or to celebrate the feast of the passover. This gives us an insight into the infinite peace and joy and victory that Christ had in his soul while on the way to death.

And then we must remember that Christ, the Son of God, is the fountain out of which has come all creation and all beauty, and all music. All the sweet songs that the angels can sing or that men can sound forth, all the melody of songbirds or of musical instruments, or the melodious breaking of the waters on the seashore, all music in all worlds, comes out of him who is the fountain of creation and the author of all truth and melody, all poetry, and all song.

John tells us that he heard the voice of Jesus like the sound of many waters. When a great billow rolls up and breaks on the seashore, it gives forth all the sounds of the octave, from the deepest bass to the highest treble; and so the voice of Jesus sounded in the ears of John like the beautiful music of many waters on the rocks of Patmos. It may be, so far as we know, that in heaven they all speak in music, and that melodious sounds will accompany the utterance of every word in the glorified state.

As the Lamb of God has gone down into the depths of all sorrows, so he will ascend into the altitudes of all possible joy; and if he, as the Scriptures tell us, groaned within himself and thereby expressed an agony which no one could tell, so, on the other hand, he will utter forth the sweetest music that can possibly be formed by infinite power and skill. We have references to this in the Song of Solomon, the witness of the bridegroom's joy, and the unutterable charm there is in the utterance of his words.

Now, the song of the Lamb celebrates the ways of God. The ways of God refer to that vast world of interior light and love and purpose and disposition inside the Divine Being.

Writers have divided the glory of God into two parts, and they speak of all of the glory which God has from his created universe as his *accidental* glory, or glory that lies, as it were, on the outside of God; and then they speak of the glory of his own perfections as his *internal* glory, or the glory that he has essentially and eternally, in himself, which is not dependent on any external creation. If there were no outward creation, God would still be absolutely perfect in every way and form and degree within himself. His power, love, wisdom, eternity, purity, sweetness, tranquility, justice, and all the perfections that we can conceive of, belong to him in an infinite degree. Now, it is this inner life of God that is revealed by the Lamb. The Son of God dwelt from eternity in the bosom of the Father, and he alone is acquainted with all the thoughts and purposes of the Father; and he alone can reveal the secret ways of the Godhead.

We can pick up a small acorn in our hands and look at it, but how little do we suspect of the ways that are coiled up in that acorn. Out of that acorn, when planted, will come the gigantic oak that will live for hundreds of years; and yet every secret way of that oak is hoarded up in that small acorn – the size of the tree, the color, the shape, the odor, the growth – all the characteristics of that giant oak are but the outward unfolding of the secret ways that lie hidden in the acorn.

We take up an eagle's egg and look at it, but how little do we suspect of all the secret ways that lie inside of that egg. Yonder, in the upper blue sky, five miles above the earth, soars the great eagle; and yet the way that that eagle flies and lives and screams and plunges and catches its game, all the habits and all the long life of that eagle which make up the way of the eagle, lie inside of the egg.

It is thus that the ways of God, which lie hidden in the radiant depths of the Godhead, are known to the Lamb and revealed by the Lamb.

Just as there are two words which characterize the song of Moses – "great" and "marvelous" – so there are two words which characterize the song of the Lamb: they are "just" and "true." The word "just" refers to the absolute righteousness of all of God's ways. They are perfectly pure and holy, free from all partiality or cruelty or crookedness, for those ways are the outcome of an infinitely holy being, and every impulse of his nature is absolutely perfect as to its origin and its manifestation. This justice of the ways of God was manifested in the death of Christ, the dying of the just for the unjust, the making of an atonement for the sins of the world, so that God could save sinners in perfect harmony with all of his perfections.

In making an atonement for the sins of mankind, Jesus manifested God's character in a way that would never have been known to the universe except through the atonement. It manifested the righteousness of God in reference to sin, in a way which never could have been manifested in wrath or in punishment upon the sinner – when God himself put the punishment of sin upon his spotless Son in order that he might be just, and yet the justifier of him that believeth.

The next word is, that they are "true," that is, faithful. This word refers to the absolute accuracy of God's covenants, that his promises are fulfilled to the uttermost without default. The fidelity of God in keeping his covenants is referred to more frequently in Scripture than any other perfection of the divine nature. It is his fidelity on which we can lean with absolute security. Solomon speaks of God performing with his hands that which he had promised with his mouth. The promises of God are based on his infinite justice, and the fulfillment of the promises is in agreement with his faithfulness.

In the period of the judgment, the glorified saints will be assembled on the glassy sea up in the sky, and every one of that countless throng will be able to bear witness that God has never broken a promise; that his faithfulness has proven true throughout all generations and under all circumstances; and thus they will celebrate in that great song the glorious fidelity of God, through his Son Jesus, in keeping the covenants of pardon and cleansing and resurrection and glorification, and in giving to his saints the inheritance of the kingdom, which was prepared for them from the foundation of the world.

The song of the Lamb will find an echo in every heart of those who are redeemed, for every one of them can look into his own life and his own personal history and see the accomplishment of God's promises in personal experience.

While the song of Moses will direct the attention of the saints to the external universe, in its magnitudes and marvelous secrets, yet the song of the Lamb will direct their attention to their own inner hearts, and to that marvelous work of grace in saving them from all sin, and bringing them into the Father's house, and crowning them with unspeakable glory.

Chapter 14

The Marriage Supper of the Lamb

AFTER the glorified saints sing their victorious song of Moses and the Lamb, standing on the sea of glass and playing on the harps of God, there follows the judgments on Babylon and on the mother of harlots, and after the false satanic woman has been judged and destroyed, then that company which makes up the bride of the Lamb appears in glorified splendor and the marriage supper is celebrated.

"And I heard the voice of a great multitude as the voice of many waters, and as the voice of mighty thunderings, saying, Hallelujah: for the Lord God omnipotent reigneth. Let us be glad and rejoice, and give honor to him: for the marriage of the Lamb is come, and his wife hath made herself ready. And to her was granted that she should be arrayed in fine linen, clean and white: for the fine linen is the righteousness of saints. And he saith unto me, Blessed are they which are called unto the marriage supper of the Lamb. And he saith unto me, These are the true sayings of God" (Rev. 19:6-9).

The time of this marriage supper is at the close of the great tribulation judgment, just before the destruction of the Antichrist and the chaining of Satan. The locality of this banquet is up in the sky, where Jesus and the glorified saints have been during the years that the great tribulation judgments were poured out on the earth.

There are two cities that are spoken of all through the Bible: Babylon and Jerusalem. Babylon is always the home of backsliders and the seat of satanic power. Jerusalem is the city of God, the true home of the saints. These two cities are always spoken of in contrast. In the final outcome, Babylon goes down like a stone

145

in the sea, into everlasting destruction, and Jerusalem is perpetuated in the New Jerusalem, the city of pure gold, the everlasting
home of the redeemed.

There are also two women that are spoken of all through
Scripture: one is typified by Jezebel, the false prophetess, and
the other is typified by Sarah, who represents the true spiritual
church, and is the mother of us all, as Paul says. In the previous
chapter of Revelation, the false woman goes down in awful judgment, and in the passage we have now before us we see the true
woman, the bride of Christ, coming forth in everlasting triumph
and radiant glory to take her place in the union with the Lord
Jesus, the Lamb, to rule forever and forever.

The word "Hallelujah" is mentioned four times in chapter
19, as expressing the perfection of praise and victory that the
great salvation has reached its final consummation. There is more
expression of joy, of gladness, over the marriage of the Lamb
than over any other event mentioned in the book of Revelation,
because it is the consummation of redemption, the fulfillment
of all promises and all prophecies concerning the victory of the
Lord Jesus and his glorified saints.

In explaining this passage, let us notice:

1. Who is the Bridegroom?

The Scriptures make it very clear that the bridegroom can be
no other person than the Lamb, the blessed Son of God, the Savior of sinners. But when we say this, let us remember that there
is a perfect fitness in the fact that the Son of God is the bridegroom, because it is by Christ that God created the universe, all
worlds, and angels, and men, and because the Son of God is the
creator of all things the universe is to be linked on to God the
Father through his Son. Now, inasmuch as Christ is that divine
person that links the creation to the Godhead, it is eminently
fitting that he should be the bridegroom.

The kingdom of Israel in the Old Testament was often spoken of as the wife of Jehovah, but the language always indicates
that the husband of Israel was the second person in the Godhead,
the Jehovah-Savior. When the prophets speak of Jehovah as the

husband of Israel, they also mention the fact that he is the Savior and the Redeemer, proving that the person was that of the Lord Jesus and not the person of the eternal Father or the person of the Holy Ghost. But remember that Israel was spoken of as the wife of Jehovah in an earthly sense, as an elect people from the nations of the earth and not as a heavenly people or as a glorified people. The Jewish nation, in crucifying the Son of God, killed its husband, and hence became a widow, and is referred to in many places as a widow. When Jesus died on the cross, he was thereby divorced from Israel, and when he arose from the dead he was free from the Israel wife and at perfect liberty to espouse another wife gathered from the Gentiles and Jews alike to form a new body, or a new bride. This is the clear teaching of Paul and Isaiah.

And again, it is of necessity that the Lamb shall be the bridegroom because he is the one that died for sinners, and purchased for himself a people from death. We are not redeemed by the person of the eternal Father or by the person of the Holy Ghost, but by the person of the Son of God, through the sacrifice of his human body, and he thereby is the proprietor of the saved ones as no other person in the Godhead is.

2. Who is the bride?

In answer to this question there are a great many different opinions, but I am sure that the Scriptures are very clear as to who they are that constitute the bride of the Lamb. In every single place in the Scripture where this subject is referred to there is a showing that the bride of Christ does not take in all those who are saved from the earth, but a chosen company who have been selected from the saved ones, because they have met certain conditions of consecration, purification and obedience, and have been thereby qualified to take rank with Christ in his rulership in the coming ages.

There are several names given to that company which constitutes the bride of Christ, such as "the church of the firstborn," "the elect," "the overcomers," and similar expressions. It is a great mistake to think that the church of the firstborn includes all who are saved from among men, for the Bible expressly indicates what is meant by the "firstborn." When the death angel passed over Egypt, the firstborn of the Hebrews were spared, and from that time on the firstborn in every family were to be entirely the Lord's. Surely all the other children belonged to God; but the firstborn were entirely his in a special way. In the wilderness, God said to Moses that he would take the tribe of Levi and sanctify them and make them for the firstborn: and instead of taking the firstborn from each family he would take Levi's tribe for the firstborn (Numbers 3:12). He said, in another place, that all the twelve tribes belonged to him, but that Levi's tribe belonged to him in a special way, to be a tribe that was holy and that should teach the other tribes the law. Paul tells us in the 12th chapter of Hebrews, that when we come to the pentecost at Mount Zion, we come to the general assembly and church of the firstborn. The general assembly embraces all who are saved from the human race, but the church of the firstborn is a selection from that countless multitude, just as Levi's tribe was a selection from the twelve tribes.

The word "elect" is applied often to the bride of Christ, but that word "elect" never refers to being saved; it always refers to the work of sanctification and to a rank that believers take after they are saved, as where Peter says, "Ye are elect through sanctification."

In the forty-fifth Psalm, David describes first the bridegroom, and in the second half of the psalm he describes the bride. He mentions other companies of saved ones and speaks of them as Kings' daughters and as honorable women; but in contrast to these companies he refers to the queen, standing at the right hand of the king, dressed in the gold of Ophir. And in the 6th chapter of the Song of Solomon he describes various companies of saved ones under the names of queens, virgins; and then refers to the elect daughter who is the bride, as being superior to them all, and says, "She is the choice one," and the word means, the elect one of all others.

Jesus refers to this select company of bridehood saints when he explained the reason why his disciples did not weep and fast, in contrast to John's disciples; because he said: "My disciples are the children of the bride chamber, and how can they weep and fast when they have the Bridegroom with them?" Hence the bride will be a company selected from the saved ones of all the ages, both Jews and Gentiles, formed into one body which will meet the conditions of heart purity and devotion to God and have thereby been qualified for that rank which will be manifested at the time of the marriage.

3. "She hath made herself ready." This preparation takes place before the wedding day comes on. Just as the judgment of the saints does not save them, but manifests their salvation and reveals the rank that each will have in the heavenly kingdom, so the bride makes herself ready during her lifetime on the earth and in the state of probation. But the fullness of the preparation is made manifest in the time of the wedding.

4. The wedding garments of the bride: "She was arrayed in fine linen, clean and white."

The word "white" should be *brilliant, radiant.* There are always three words used in describing the condition or character of the victorious saints. One word refers to justification, and the next refers to sanctification, and the third refers to the enduring of tests and trials by which the soul is made radiant and luminous, or radiant and glorious. Daniel says that the company shall be purified, made white, and tried; that is, have their sins washed out, and then made white in purity, and then tried to test and prove their obedience. In this passage, the expression "fine linen" refers to justification, the forgiveness of sins; and the word "clean" refers to purity, to holiness; and the word "white" refers to being tested in the fire, and made radiant in the glory of a victorious experience. The word "righteous" is, in the original, in the plural number, and the passage should read, "for the fine linen is the righteousnesses of the saints." There is a righteousness that is obtained in justification, and there is a righteousness that is inwrought in the heart by the Holy Spirit: and then there is a righteousness that is wrought out in the believer's life in obedience and good works. The Scriptures speak of the soul being clothed by its character. The wicked are driven away in their sins: that is, clothed, covered, with their sins as a raiment. Also the righteous are spoken of as clothed with the garments of salvation. When the saints are glorified they will be clothed in light, such as the angels wear and such as Jesus wore after his resurrection. But just as there are degrees of rewards and of ranks in the kingdom of heaven, so there will be great degrees in the size and luster of the garments that the glorified saints will wear; and David says that the queen, the Lamb's wife, will be dressed in the gold of Ophir, and in another place it says that her garments are of wrought gold. It is in sanctification that the soul becomes espoused to Christ, but the marriage does not take place until the resurrection, when the saints are caught up to meet the Lord in the air, and pass judgment, and receive their rewards.

We should notice that in this Scripture we are not told of what the marriage ceremony will consist. That is a subject that has not been clearly revealed, though it is hinted at in several places in the Bible. We know that marriage means union, and Jesus says, "They two shall be one flesh." And this perfect union will be accomplished in a divine and transcendent manner, surpassing all our earthly conceptions.

When Moses dedicated the tabernacle, God came down and filled the tent with his glory so that no priest could enter the sanctuary. Also, when Solomon dedicated the temple, God filled the temple with his glory, and no man could enter the holy places on that occasion. These instances furnish us with a hint as to the marriage of the Lamb with his elect bride, that it will be an outpouring of a flood of glory and a rapturous oneness with the Son of God in a glorified state – the consummation of so many promises bearing on that subject.

Let us now consider the supper or the banquet which will celebrate the marriage. "Blessed are they which are called unto the marriage of the Lamb." Let us set it in our faith that, according to the Word of God, this will be a real supper, a real feast of eating and drinking just as literally as we eat and drink in this life. Those who represent this supper as only a metaphor or an illustration or as a parable grossly misrepresent the Word of God, which means exactly what it says in this connection or it means nothing at all.

This great feast has been prophesied all through the Scriptures, in both the Old and the New Testament, and is always spoken of as a veritable eating and drinking. Abraham entertained three heavenly beings in his tent in Beersheba, and one of them was the Jehovah, the Son of God, and all three of them ate and drank the dinner that Abraham prepared for them. The Lord Jesus ate and drank after his resurrection just as positively as before he died, and he was certainly in his glorified body at the time that he partook of the food on the shore of the lake, and on other occasions.

The Scriptures tell us that the manna that God gave the Israelites was the food of the angels; and it only shows self-conceited infidelity when persons deny that Word. When Jesus gave the Last Supper, on the night of his betrayal, he passed the cup of wine to his disciples and said, "Drink ye all of this, but I will not drink it until I drink it new with you in my Father's kingdom." And in another place he said, "I will not drink of the fruit of the vine," meaning: literally grape juice, "until I drink it with you in my Father's kingdom." This proves absolutely that the eating and drinking at the marriage supper of the Lamb will be as literal and positive as it was that last night when they ate the supper together.

In the writings of Moses it was commanded that anybody could take the vow of a Nazarite for any length of time that he pleased – for a month, or a year, or a number of years; but it was stipulated that during the length of time of the Nazarite vow, the man should not taste any product of the vine; should not eat the grape, nor drink the juice; but that, when the time of the vow expired, the man could then drink the juice and eat the fruit of the vine. This explains the words of Jesus. Christ had been drinking grape juice all through his life, but on the night of the Last Supper he took the vow of the Nazarite, which was to extend throughout the entire period of the church age until his second coming. And at the time of judgment, when the marriage of the Lamb will take place, that vow will then have expired, and then he will be free again to drink of the fruit of the vine. This shows clearly that Christ will drink with his glorified saints the fruit of the vine just as truly as he had been drinking it all through his previous life.

There is another suggestion that should be mentioned in this connection, and that is, the wonderful sacredness of eating and drinking as expressed throughout all Scripture from beginning to end. In the sight of God, eating and drinking constitutes a blessed sacrament. If you will study the significance of the eating of fruit in the Garden of Eden, and of the command not to eat of the Tree of Knowledge, and then notice the change of diet given to Noah and his sons after the flood, that they could eat meat, and then the eating of the passover lamb in Egypt, and then Moses and the seventy elders eating and drinking in the presence of God up in Mount Sinai, and then the heavenly visitors eating and drinking with Abraham, and then the eating and drinking at the Last Supper, and then the eating and drinking with Christ after his resurrection, and the institution of the Lord's Supper – the eating of bread and the drinking of grape juice to be kept up as a memorial until the second coming of Christ, and then this great banquet in the heavens at the time of the marriage of the Lamb – all these and many other Scriptures show us that there must be a divine significance in eating and drinking, as a holy sacrament which we have never yet fully understood or appreciated.

Now let us notice that great company of guests that are called to the marriage supper of the Lamb. It is very plain that these invited guests are not the bride, neither can the words be construed to signify that they are the angels; but they are human beings, saved men and women, who have been redeemed and resurrected from the dead, and are invited to take part with Christ and his bride at the marriage supper. In the forty-fifth Psalm, after describing the bride, the queen, and saying that she is brought unto the King in raiment of fine needlework, it is then mentioned that the virgins, her companions that follow her, shall be brought in also, and that with gladness and rejoicing shall these virgins be brought in, and that they shall enter into the King's palace (Psa. 45:14-15). From these words it is as plain as day that these virgins are not the bride, but that they are her companions. They follow after her; they are brought as guests into the King's palace and partake of the banquet: but the bride is the queen of the palace and co-regent with the King himself. John described one company, in Revelation, as living creatures, and then elders with gold crowns on their heads, who are in the throne and round about the throne, and as having been saved from all nations and kindreds and tongues, and as taking part with Christ in the functions of judgment and of government; and then afterwards he speaks of a company which no man can number, gathered from all nations, standing before the throne, with white robes, and palms in their hands; but they have no crowns on their heads, and they are not in the throne like the living creatures and the elders, but are standing before the throne. All these are redeemed by the same Savior and washed in the same blood, but they do not all have the same rank. But these countless millions are all invited as guests to the marriage supper.

All these things are accomplished in the life and experience of Christians in this present life to some degree. For example, it is the bridehood saints that start revivals and push the work of saving souls, and establishing missions, and that take the initiative in all religious work; and when their labors are accomplished, by the power of the Holy Spirit, all other believers come in and share the blessings and benefits, though they are not the leaders in the work of God, and occupy a secondary place in faith and spiritual zeal. They correspond to the guests at the banquet. In every religious movement of the Christian faith, from the days of the apostles down to this present time, there have always been those who were front rank believers, and who were leaders in all movements of revival and mission work; and these are those that correspond to the bridehood saints. And besides these there have always been large numbers gathered into the church that became believers and trusted in Christ for salvation and had a measure of the Spirit of God, but who never possessed that measure of faith and zeal to put them in the front rank, but who yet shared in the benefits that God gave to the front rank saints.

A picture of this is set forth in the call of Rebecca to be the wife of Isaac. When Abraham's servant met Rebecca at the well, he gave her a ring from Isaac, which was a type of justification and of her acceptance. But later on, in the home, when she agreed to leave father and mother, and brothers and sisters, and home and country, to go to a distant land and be the wife of Isaac, the servant then brought out large gifts and bestowed them upon her because she had accepted the position of a bride, and those large gifts typify the full baptism of the Holy Spirit which a believer receives when he becomes espoused to be the bride of Jesus.

Now it is said that at that very time the servant of Abraham, in addition to these great gifts to Rebecca, gave gifts also to all the members of the family. Laban and his wife and the brothers and sisters and all the members of the family shared in the bounty of Isaac. This is exactly what is set forth in many other Scriptures, that the millions of saved ones who are not in the bridehood, and who are the guests at the wedding, will also share in the boundless blessings which are given to the bride by the divine Bridegroom.

Another suggestion is found in the fact that those saints who are not in the bridehood company will admire the bride and praise her for having been counted worthy to obtain her rank. It is said that the name of the bride will be remembered in all generations forever and ever (Psa. 45:17).

Another passage to the same effect is found in the Song of Solomon 6:9, that when the wedding takes place the daughters – that is, those who are not in the bridehood – will see the bride and will bless her, and that the queens – that is, those who have high rank in the kingdom, but who are not the bride – will praise her.

In this life, the bridehood saints are criticized and persecuted on account of their intense devotion, and because they pursue holiness of heart and life and because of their deadness to this present world; and because of their zeal for holy and heavenly things they are misunderstood and misrepresented, and often persecuted not only by sinners but by great multitudes of Christian people. But in the time of the kingdom, when the wedding takes place, then the bridehood saints will come into their own, and the very people on earth and in the churches that criticized and persecuted the true saints of God will see things in their true light in the heavenly world, and then they will praise the bridehood saints, and honor them because of their excellence in the life of Christ. A picture of this is found in the life of Job, that after he went through his great sufferings, God made the three friends that persecuted him go to him and confess their fault, and get Job to pray for them, and also it is said that his brethren and sisters and kinfolks came to Job after his trials were over, and brought many gifts of gold and silver and jewels, and they then expressed their appreciation of Job's marvelous faith and character. This is what will take place up in heaven at the time of the marriage banquet. All of the saved ones who do not take rank in this present life sufficient to put them in the bridehood company will, at that day, praise the elect saints and fully appreciate their worth in the great plan which God has carried out in redemption.

Chapter 15

The White Horse Army

IN tracing the history of the glorified saints, the very next thing after the marriage supper of the Lamb is the sublime wedding tour, when the Bridegroom and his bride, with the countless millions of attendants, mount their white horses of fire, and descend to this earth to take possession of the estate of rulership over the world, which was forfeited by Adam and redeemed again by the Lamb of God, and all the old usurpers who have run the world for six thousand years will be utterly displaced, and the estate of the world will revert to the original heirs who will take possession and rule over it forever. This event is described in the following passage:

"And I saw heaven opened, and behold a white horse: and he that sat upon him was called Faithful and True, and in righteousness he doth judge and make war. His eyes were as a flame of fire, and on his head were many crowns; and he had a name written that no man knew, but he himself. And he was clothed with a vesture dipped in blood: and his name is called The Word of God. And the armies which were in heaven followed him upon white horses, clothed in fine linen, white and clean" (Rev. 19:11-14).

To form a clear conception of this passage, let us remember that in chapter 4, John saw a door opened in heaven and at the opening of that door the sound of a trumpet was heard, which is the trumpet of the first resurrection, and a voice saying, "Come up hither." The first opening of the door in heaven is for the rapture of the saints, to take up the resurrected righteous and to catch away the living righteous that they may meet the Lord together in the air. But the second opening of the door in heaven is for the purpose of the revelation, the full and perfect and open manifestation of Christ and the glorified saints back to this world.

There are two sets of Scriptures referring to the second coming of the Lord. One set of passages speaks of the catching away of the saints up into heaven, and the other set of passages speaks of their return with the Lord Jesus back to this earth. Let me give you a few passages on the rapture· of the saints:

Psa. 50:3-5: "Our God shall come and he shall call to the heavens from above, and to the earth, and say: Gather my saints together unto me; those that have made a covenant with me by sacrifice." Here we see that the coming of God is mentioned in connection with the gathering of the saints together to meet him in the air.

In Luke 17:34-37, we read: "I tell you, in that night there shall be two in one bed; the one shall be taken, and the other left. Two shall be grinding together; the one shall be taken, and the other left. Two shall be in the field; the one shall be taken, and the other left. And the disciples said, Where, Lord, will they be taken? And he said unto them, Wheresoever the body" (that is, the body of Christ) "is, thither will the eagles" (that is, the eagle saints) "be gathered together." This Scripture does not refer to the destruction of Jerusalem, for the words were not accomplished then of one being taken and the other left; neither do these words refer to Christ's returning to the earth, but emphatically they refer to the picking up of the prepared saints, suddenly from the earth, to be with the glorified body of Christ in the sky.

Again, Jesus says, in John 14:3, "I go to prepare a place for you; and if I go and prepare a place for you I will come again and receive you unto myself, that where I am there ye may be also." This is most explicit on the rapture, or the catching away of the saints when Jesus comes to gather them.

Another passage is found in 2 Thes. 2:1: "Now we beseech you, brethren, by the coming of our Lord Jesus Christ, and by our gathering together unto him."

All these passages and many more set forth the doctrine of the rapture, this being caught up to meet Christ in heaven. And they will remain with Christ while the tribulation is going on upon the earth, and after the wedding supper will return, riding upon white horses.

Now, in the next place, let me show a few Scriptures on the return of the saints back to the earth after the marriage feast. The passage which I have given from Rev. 19 is just as explicit as language could make it, that the saints are to return with Christ from the wedding. But there are other passages which agree with the one in the text. In Psalm 126:6 we read: "He that goeth forth and weepeth, bearing precious seed, shall doubtless come again with rejoicing, bringing his sheaves with him." This shows that there is to be a second coming of the saints back to this earth just as truly as there is to be a second coming of Christ. In this same world, where the servants of God have wept, and sown their precious seed and toiled in the church age, after being received up into heaven and passing their judgment, they are to come back again to this earth with great rejoicing, bringing their sheaves, their rewards and honors that they have acquired, back to this earth with them.

In Isaiah 64 we read: "Oh that thou wouldst rend the heavens, that thou wouldst come down, that the mountains might bow down at thy presence, as when the melting fire burneth, the fire causeth the waters to boil, to make thy name known to thine adversaries, that the nations may tremble at thy presence!" This passage does not refer to the rapture, but to the open Apocalypse when Christ will rend the heavens, or, as Saint John says, open a door in heaven, and descend, with melting fire, and all the nations of the earth who have been going through their tribulation judgment will tremble at his return.

In the 7th chapter of Daniel we read: "I beheld till the thrones were cast down" (that is, all earthly governments destroyed) "and the Ancient of days did sit; his throne was like the fiery flame, and a fiery stream issued and came forth from before him; thousand thousands ministered unto him, and ten thousand times ten thousand stood before him. And I beheld till the beast" (that is, the Antichrist) "was slain and his body destroyed and given to the burning flame, and I saw one like the Son of man come with the clouds of heaven, and there was given him dominion and glory and a kingdom, that all people, nations and languages should serve him."

When Jesus comes to catch away his saints, it is said he will come as a thief, but when he returns with all his saints, he will come with flames of fire, and it is at that time that every eye shall see him and all nations shall wail because of him.

The apostle Paul speaks of having our hearts established in holiness before God at the coming of our Lord Jesus Christ *with all his saints* (1 Thes. 3:13). And again, the apostle says that the Lord Jesus Christ shall be revealed from *heaven* with his mighty angels and flaming fire, taking vengeance on them that obey not the gospel, who shall be punished with everlasting destruction from the presence of the Lord and from the glory of his power, when he shall come to be glorified in his saints and to be admired in all them that believe in that day (2 Thes. 1:7-10).

And again we read: "Behold the Lord cometh with ten thousands of his saints to execute judgment upon all, and to convince all that are ungodly among them of their ungodly deeds which they have ungodly committed" (Jude 14-15). These are a few among the many portions of Scripture which refer especially to Christ's coming after the saints are glorified and receive their rewards and pass through the experience of the marriage supper of the Lamb.

The next point to be considered is the person of Christ as revealed in his descent on the white horse. Let us remember that every single passage in the Bible which describes Christ always represents him in connection with the occasion and the circumstance and the relation in which he is revealed. When he is spoken of as a high priest, he is always spoken of in terms and as arrayed in garments that specially become the functions of a priest. When he is spoken of as a sacrifice and a suffering Savior, the language is always appropriate to that subject, as the slain

Lamb, as a sacrificial offering, as making an atonement for the sins of the world.

When he is spoken of as a king, the language used and the circumstances always harmonize with a monarch on his throne, with scepter and crown and similar belongings. When he is spoken of as a bridegroom, the description always agrees with the special function. In this passage he is pre-eminently described as a warrior returning to this earth to make war on the Antichrist and all the armies who have on them the mark of the beast, to slay them and consign their leader to the lake of fire. Hence every word in the passage we are considering agrees with the presentation of the Lord Jesus in that capacity. For this reason, we do not find the word "Lamb," or the word "Jesus" used in the passage, because he is coming in the capacity of a great warrior to take vengeance on his enemies, and the words "Lamb," or "Jesus" would not be in consonance with that office. In the previous verses, when the wedding was referred to he was spoken of as the Lamb, because that title is the one to be used in connection with his marriage to the elect saints who have been prepared to be his bride. It will help you to understand the Scriptures better if you will keep this thought in mind in all your Bible reading – that each description given to Christ agrees with the circumstances and with the work to be done by him.

For six thousand years this world has been under the usurpation of the enemies of God, and with all the boasted civilizations, improvements and education and the multiplied religions in the world, the human race has constantly degenerated and the human heart grown more obdurate, proud, self-willed, until the race culminates in bowing down to Antichrist and worshiping that great beast in the place of God. This will be the climax to the history of sin and natural human character, and the time will then be perfectly ripe for the Son of God, as a divine warrior, to return, armed with omnipotent righteousness and with a sharp sword proceeding out of his mouth, in order that he may destroy his enemies and assume absolute command of the world which he has bought with his own blood. It is in that last great conflict that the garments which Christ wears will be dipped in the blood of his enemies. This is what is described in Isaiah 63: "Who is this that cometh from Edom with dyed garments from Bozrah? this that is glorious in his apparel, traveling in the greatness of his strength? Wherefore art thou red in thine apparel, and thy garments like him that treadeth in the winefat? I have trodden the winepress alone; for I will tread down mine enemies in mine anger, and trample them in my fury; and their blood shall be sprinkled upon my garments, and I will stain all my raiment. For the day of vengeance is in mine heart, and the year of my redeemed is come. And I will tread down the people in mine anger, and make them drunk in my fury, and I will bring down their strength to the earth" (Isaiah 63:1-6).

How foolish it is for anyone to apply this Scripture to down on the white horse. Calvary and Bozrah are just the crucifixion of Christ. Jesus was never in Bozrah in all his life, but he will descend over Bozrah when he comes exactly the opposites. Calvary is where Christ shed his blood, but Bozrah is where the armies of the Antichrist will shed their blood. On Calvary Jesus shed his blood on his enemies, but at Bozrah he will sprinkle his garments with the blood of his enemies. Calvary was at the opening of the church age, but Bozrah will be at the last great battle which closes the church age. On Calvary Jesus had no vengeance, but he prayed for his Father to forgive his murder; but at Bozrah will be the time of divine vengeance on the Lord's enemies. If each portion of Scripture could be rightly placed in relationship to time and dispensation, it would give people great light in understanding the different ages and dispensations of revealed truth.

The sword that this divine warrior will use in slaying his enemies is not made of steel, but it is a word-sword, infinitely more powerful than any sword made of iron. The Word of God can kill or can make alive with omnipotent and instantaneous power. Jesus, in the Garden of Gethsemane, spoke in a mild tone of voice saying that he was Jesus, and yet one hundred strong Roman soldiers, when they heard his word, went backward and fell to the ground as if struck with a cannon ball, which is only one instance of the omnipotence there is in the outspoken word of the Lord Jesus when he comes in judgment.

The next item to be considered in the passage is that of the army of the glorified saints following the divine warrior, riding on white horses and clothed in fine linen, clean and dazzling. You notice the word "armies" is in the plural number, because, as the Scriptures abundantly show, there are a great many ranks and degrees of redeemed human beings in the kingdom of heaven. According to Saint John, the highest rank of saved men is represented by the typical number of the four living creatures, and the next rank is represented by the twenty-four elders with golden crowns. These two classes are spoken of as being in the throne and round about the throne, sitting on thrones in connection with the enthroned Lamb. The next rank of saved ones is spoken of as the hundred and forty-four thousand who are the first fruit in the great restoration of Israel. The next army of saints is spoken of as a multitude that no man can number, standing before the throne, having no crowns on their heads but having palms in their hands. The next rank of saved ones is spoken of as the nations of those who are saved. Hence we see that the countless millions of those who are saved of the human race will form distinct ranks and distinct armies. The bridehood saints rank the highest, next to the King of Glory himself, for they are the chosen company, out from the body, who have specially qualified themselves to be the queen of the Son of God. Just as God, in forming Eve, did not take the whole body of Adam, but only a rib from the center of his body, so the bride is that company selected as a rib from the great body that is formed of redeemed people.

These bridehood saints follow next to Christ on white horses, and then follow other armies, spoken of in one place as virgins without number, according to their various degrees. All these glorified armies of saved people will come riding down from the sky, from the marriage supper, following the Lord Jesus on horses of white fire, to take part with Christ in the destruction of the armies of the Antichrist, and to take part with him in ruling the nations with a rod of iron, or, more properly, "shepherdizing the nations with inflexible righteousness," typified by the rod of iron.

To make this a little more real to our understanding, let us remember that the Scripture teaches that God forms horses of fire just as truly and literally as he forms horses of grass or dust. Every reference to horses and chariots of fire in the Bible is most positively spoken of in connection with men, saved men from the earth, as truly as of angels. Elijah went up into heaven in a chariot of fire drawn by horses of fire, and those horses were made of fire as literally as our horses are made of dust, for it is just as easy for God to make a horse out of white fire as out of grass or dust. Another instance is where the prophet Elisha was in Dothan and surrounded by the armies of the Assyrians, and he saw the mountains around the city full of chariots and horses of fire. We have in the book of Judges the account of a battle which was led by Deborah and Barak against the armies of Israel, and it is said that the stars in their courses fought against the enemies of God, which proves that there is such a thing as supernatural armies in the spirit world that God uses when he pleases to defeat his enemies or protect his saints.

The glorified saints will share in the very feelings which Christ has toward the enemies of God, and in the winding up of this present world's history these saints are to be endowed with judgment authority over the world and take part with Christ in judging the world and in overthrowing all the systems of iniquity, and in ridding the world of its tyrants and usurpers. This is described in Psalm 149, where we read: "Let the saints be joyful in glory, and let the high praises of God be in their mouths, and a two-edged sword in their hands, to execute vengeance against the heathen and punishment against the people" (that is, the armies of the Antichrist) "to bind their kings with chains and their nobles with fetters of iron, to execute upon them the judgment that is written in the prophecy; and this honor have all saints." This Scripture does not apply to the servants of God in the present dispensation, for we are now living in the age of the cross, in the age of humiliation and suffering and persecution and the various testings of our faith and love. But this Scripture belongs to the age of the crown and the kingdom and the glory and the dominion which is to be ushered in after the resurrection of the righteous.

You must distinguish between those words in the Bible which belong to the age of the cross and those other Scriptures which belong to the age of the crown. It is very awkward when people try to make the Scriptures fit into a period for which they are not intended. When Peter drew his sword and cut off the ear of the high priest's servant, Jesus told Peter to put up his sword, because that was the period when Christ and his saints were to suffer the indignities of the wicked, and that age of patient endurance still continues. But when the saints come riding down with Christ on white horses made of fire, that will be the age of judgment, of the righteous wrath of God against all wickedness, and in that age the glorified saints will act in harmony with the wrath of God, just as truly as in this present age they act in harmony with the long-suffering and patience of God.

Many of the ablest Bible expositors and the most godly saints in past generations have believed that God will raise from the dead those horses which have been very useful to men in this life, and glorify those horses and continue to use them in the coming ages for the saints to ride upon. That may be true, or may not, but one thing is certain: everything belongs to God, and he has the absolute right and law and power to resurrect any dead creature that he pleases, and use it in any way he may choose for his glory, and he will not stop to consult the higher critics or an infidel church or an ungodly world as to what he may do in the glorious age that is to come. He can either resurrect dead creatures, or form creatures by his omnipotence out of white fire, and do the one thing just as easily as the other. We know nothing of the various modes by which God may operate, but we do know that his Word is infallibly inspired, and that every word written by the Holy Ghost will be fulfilled at the proper time and in the proper way.

This descent of the white horse army will be the time when all those Scriptures will be fulfilled about the saints coming into their inheritance which has so long been promised to them, and taking possession of those estates which have been forfeited to their enemies through so many centuries. All such prophecies are in connection with a time of judgment. There is no place in Scripture that says the saints are to get possession of this world by a slow and easy and peaceful process, because Satan and the Antichrist and their armies will contend for the mastery of the world to the last point; and it is always a time of judgment and wrath and outpoured punishment when the world is to be conquered and the saints get possession by a divine conflict and the overthrow of the adversary. How striking are the words of the prophet that Israel shall be redeemed with judgment. That truth not only applies to the twelve tribes of Israel being restored in the judgment tribulation, but it is a key Scripture, that the possession of this world by the righteous will take place in a time of judgment, and Isaiah says it will be in the day of the great slaughter. And Jesus says that when he returns, after judging the saints, he will say: "Where are those mine enemies that would not let me rule over them? Bring them before me and slay them in my presence." The judgment wrath of God against this wicked world is not a metaphor nor a piece of poetry, but an awful reality; and nothing is more plainly taught in Scripture than the coming wrath of God and the last great conflict with the hosts of sin. And when that battle closes, with victory for Jesus and his white horse army, then, and only then, will war cease forever on this earth.

CHAPTER 16

The Destruction of Antichrist

THERE are two great events that are to follow immediately upon the return of Christ with his glorified saints back to the earth. The first is the destruction of the Antichrist and his armies, and the second is the chaining of Satan, which completes the removal from this earth of all forces antagonistic to Christ and prepares the way for his thousand-year reign upon the earth.

Having noticed the progressive steps in the progress and destiny of the saints, we have now come to the time of the destruction of the great Antichrist and his armies, which is described in Rev. 19:15-21. But in order to fully grasp the magnitude of this awful event, we should have a clear, scriptural view of the Antichrist himself, as to who he is and his origin and character and destiny.

There are a great number of passages in Scripture which refer to the Antichrist; but there are three special portions of the Word which more fully describe him than any others. The first passage is found in Daniel 11:36-37: "And the king shall do according to his will; and he shall exalt himself and magnify himself above every god, and shall speak marvelous things against the God of gods, and shall prosper till the indignation be accomplished: for that that is determined shall be done. Neither shall he regard the God of his fathers, nor the desire of women, nor regard any god: for he shall magnify himself above all." This remarkable passage describes a personality such as never yet has existed on this earth, and one of the most extraordinary persons and tyrants that ever has been known.

The second passage is found in 2 Thess. 2:3-10, where the apostle says that Christ will not return till there comes a falling away first, or apostasy of the church, "and that man of sin be revealed, the son of perdition; who opposeth and exalteth himself above all that is called God, or that is worshiped; so that he as God sitteth in the temple of God, showing himself that he is God. And now ye know what withholdeth (or hinders) that he might be revealed in his time. For the mystery of iniquity doth already work: only he who now letteth (or hinders) will hinder, until he be taken out of the way. And then shall that wicked (that is, Antichrist) be revealed, whom the Lord shall consume with the spirit of his mouth, and shall destroy with the brightness of his coming: even him whose coming is after the working of Satan with all power and signs and lying wonders (or deceiving miracles)." This passage agrees exactly with the passage quoted from Daniel.

The third passage describing the Antichrist, and which is the last, and, in some respects, the most complete passage on the subject, is found in Rev. 13:1-8: "And I stood upon the sands of the sea, and saw a beast rise up out of the sea, having seven heads and ten horns, and upon his horns ten crowns, and upon his head the name of blasphemy. And the beast which I saw was like unto a leopard, and his feet were as the feet of a bear, and his mouth as the mouth of a lion: and the dragon (that is, Satan) gave him power and his throne, and great authority. And I saw one of his heads as it were wounded to death: and his deadly wound was healed: and all the world wondered (that is, went into admiration) after the beast. And they worshiped the dragon (that is, Satan) which gave power unto the beast: and they worshiped the beast, saying: Who is like unto the beast? who is able to make war with him? And there was given unto him a mouth speaking great things and blasphemies: and power was given unto him to continue forty and two months (that is, three and a half years). And he opened his mouth in blasphemy against God and it was given unto him to make war with the saints, and to overcome them: and power was given him over all kindreds, and tongues and nations. And all that dwell upon the earth shall worship him, whose names are not written in the book of life of the Lamb slain from the foundation of the world."

The Scriptures teach us that there is a trinity of hell corresponding to the trinity of heaven, and that Satan is a counterfeit of God the Father, and the Antichrist is a counterfeit of the Lord Jesus, and the false prophet is a counterfeit of the Holy Spirit. And these three characters are spoken of in Scripture as attempting to counterfeit the various actions of the three persons in the divine Trinity. In the book of Revelation, Satan is described as coming down from the air, and the Antichrist is described as coming up out of the sea, and the false prophet is described as another beast, in Rev. 13:11, coming up out of the earth. There is wonderful significance in the three places from which their three personalities come. Man is composed of a trinity of spirit, soul, and body, and the spirit of man corresponds to the air, the soul of man corresponds to the sea, and the body of man corresponds to the earth.

1. Notice the time that this great Antichrist will be revealed – or, as the word signifies, have his apocalypse, for that is the word in the original. The apostle tells us in Thessalonians that the Antichrist cannot be revealed until that which hinders him is taken out of the way – which is the true spiritual church in which the Holy Spirit dwells. As long as the true spiritual church remains in the world the Antichrist cannot be manifested. The flood could not begin until Noah and his family were shut up in the ark, and Sodom could not be burned until Lot had made his escape; and in like manner the saints of the Lord must be first called away from this earth to meet Christ up in the air before the great tribulation begins and before the Antichrist can be manifested. While this is true, yet the principles of Antichrist are at work in society and in the professed church all through the gospel dispensation. This is what Paul means in saying: "The mystery of iniquity doth already work." The word "mystery" means anything which cannot be clearly known until it is revealed – that is, it cannot be distinctly ascertained by science or human learning, but must be divinely revealed in order to be perfectly understood. The mystery that Paul refers to is that the greatest iniquity that the world has ever seen or will ever see is to

exist under the guise and in the name of religion. According to Scripture, the Antichrist will be the perfection, the culmination, the climax, of all the sin of the universe bound into the one bundle of a living man, and that this perfection of all the sins of the universe will be in the name of religion, for the Antichrist will assume to be the most religious man that ever lived. This is what is meant by the mystery of iniquity, and this mystery is at work, like a satanic leaven all through the church of the gospel age, and it will ripen and burst forth in full power after the true church is called up to meet the Lord in the air.

2. This great Antichrist will be an individual man, and not a system or a theory or a nationality or a doctrine. It has been held for many years past that the Antichrist is a system, such as Romish popery or Mohammedanism, and some other things, but it is impossible to make any system on earth fit in with the words that are used in Scripture, just as it is impossible to take the skin of an elephant and make it fit a dog. All of the names given to the Antichrist refer to him as an individual person and not as a system, such as "the man of sin," "the self-willed man," "the idol shepherd," – that is, the shepherd that assumes to be God and demands that he should be worshiped. He is also called "the king," and "the prince," and the "son of perdition," and "the Antichrist." But Christ was a person, and no one can be an Antichrist, or a counterfeit Christ, without being as truly a person as Christ was. In the next place, all of his acts are such as belong to an individual person. He blasphemes, he persecutes, he disregards the desire of women, he claims worship, he changes times, he enacts laws. He performs all the acts of a tyrant or a king.

And then the time of his dominion cannot be applied to a system, or to a nation, or to a series of popes and governments. The period of the great tribulation will last about forty years, but the Antichrist does not arise until toward the close of the great tribulation, and he occupies the last seven years of that judgment time. According to Daniel, when he first arises he will make a covenant with the Jews and get them to accept him as their Messiah, and for three and a half years he will be the most plausible potentate that ever lived on earth. But in the middle of the week of years – that is, after three and a half years according to Daniel – he will break his covenant, and then, in the last three and a half years of that week of years, he will turn out to be the beast, the most awful monster of iniquity that the creation has ever beheld. Now, the length of his beastly reign of three and a half years cannot be applied to any nation or system of popery and can only be predicted of an individual man.

In the next place, the Antichrist is worshiped as a God, which cannot be applied to any nation or to a system or to a series of historical characters.

In the next place, he is cast alive into the lake of fire, which cannot be true of a nation or a system or a doctrine, for people are cast into hell as individuals. Thus every reference to the Antichrist in the Scriptures assumes him to be an individual man, and no other interpretation will possibly fit in with the Bible terms that are used.

3. According to every description of the Antichrist in Scripture he will be a supernatural character, with a constitution and an origin and a revelation and a power and a destiny above and beyond that of any other man in the entire human race. According to the words of Saint John, he will be a man that has been slain and supernaturally brought to life again. He is spoken of as the little horn that is wounded to death, and then his deadly wound is healed and he is brought to life again, and by this very supernatural restoration to life he convinces the world that he is the Messiah, and all the world goes wild in admiration of him and worships him as a god. It is said in two places that this beast ascendeth up out of the bottomless pit (Rev. 11:7, and Rev. 17:8). The bottomless pit is, in the Greek, abyss, which means the hollow place in the center of our earth; he was a man that had lived on the earth and had been slain, and his soul had gone down into the abyss and remained there until the time of the great tribulation judgment when he came up from the abyss, and his body is raised again and he makes a sudden and startling revelation to the world in imitation of the apocalypse of the Lord Jesus Christ.

This Antichrist and the false prophet are the only two human beings that ever go into the abyss and come up again out of it. According to the Bible, all the other wicked men, when they die, their spirits go to Hades, which is also located inside of this earth but not at the center. The Word of God is very explicit on this point, that Satan and the Antichrist and the false prophet are the three great personalities that go down into the abyss and come up again from the abyss, and also with them that vast army of demons which Jude tells us is now in chains until the time of the judgment, and they will be let loose to torment men under the reign of the Antichrist.

4. The Antichrist will be endowed with the most extraordinary gifts of any man that has ever lived in the world. We are told that Satan will give him all his power and his throne and all his authority, so that he will be endowed with all of the powers and attributes of the fallen archangel. He will be endowed with all of the learning, the arts, the poetry, the eloquence, the warlike gifts, the financial skill, and all other capabilities and attributes of the greatest men that have ever lived all put together, so that he will be the ideal man of this fallen world, the perfection of everything that the natural Adamic man requires.

5. The Antichrist will have a sudden apocalypse to the world to imitate the apocalypse of Christ. You notice in the passage, that he comes up from the sea a full-fledged monarch of the world, and in his dominion there is combined all of the four beasts that Daniel saw, which represent the four great monarchies of the worldwide dominion, not as a slow growth of kingdoms, but a full and perfect manifestation of all earthly kingdoms in a climax, suddenly revealed. In harmony with this, we never read anywhere in Scripture of the birth or the childhood of the Antichrist, for he is always referred to as appearing as a full-grown man in all the perfection of royal power, which is in harmony with the truth that he had previously been born, and lived and died; and then arose again as a full-sized man.

The names given to the Antichrist are very significant, as indicating the progress of his manifestation. He is first called "the king," and then "the prince," and then "the self-willed man," and then "the idol shepherd," and then "the lawless one," and then "the Antichrist," and then "the son of perdition," and "the man of sin," and at last he is called: "the beast"; and the Greek word is *therion,* which means a wild, savage beast. Thus we see that his names agree with the fact that during the first half of the seven years he acted the part of a proper king, but that at last he turns out to be the most ravenous beast in character that has ever lived on earth and the perfection of the work of the devil in mankind. The true Christ is the God-man, that is, God coming down and incarnating himself in man. The Antichrist, on the other hand, is the man-god – that is, the man that seeks to make a god of himself. Hence the Antichrist will put himself in the temple of God and deny that there is any other god in the universe than himself.

Of all the millions of human beings born of Adam's race, there is one man, and only one man, who has ever lived in whom all the points of the Antichrist will agree and that is King Saul. In a similar way, all the points in Scripture referring to the false prophet unite in the person of Judas Iscariot.

Please note the following points about the Antichrist and King Saul. In the first place, the Antichrist must be a Jew, because no Christ was ever promised to this world except from the seed of Abraham, Isaac and Jacob, and the false Christ must prove his pedigree from those ancestors in order to convince the world that he is Messiah. King Saul was a Jew, or rather, a descendant of Abraham, Isaac and Jacob. In the next place, the Antichrist will be a backslider. Satan is himself a fallen archangel and Judas is a fallen man; and the Bible speaks of Satan and Saul and Judas as all three falling, either from grace or from office; and the Antichrist will be in a special way the child of the devil, or the man who has turned away from God and accepted of the devil in place of God.

In the next place, the Antichrist will be admired by the whole world as the most consummate man they have ever known, and this agrees with what is said of King Saul. When Saul was brought forth to be crowned king, it is said that he was head and shoulders above all other men, and it is added that he was the goodliest man in all Israel; that is, the most handsome, the most magnificent in appearance, the most royal and captivating in body and manner, of any man in all Israel.

In the days of Saul the Hebrew race was the best looking people on the earth, the handsomest in form and face of all the nations, and yet King Saul was the finest looking man in the finest looking race on earth, and this will agree with what in the Scriptures is spoken of the beast – that all the world admired him.

In the fourth place, it is said that the Antichrist is a king. Daniel and Isaiah both speak of him as a king; and Saul was a king. The false prophet will be a preacher and apostle: but the Antichrist is pre-eminently a royal personage.

In the fifth place, the Antichrist will usurp all authority on earth and set up a religion and a worship of his own, trampling down all other religious authorities. This agrees exactly with what King Saul did at Gilgal. Samuel told Saul to wait for him there, and that when Samuel got there he would offer sacrifice: but King Saul grew impatient and decided to ignore the words of the prophet, and he seized the religious performances in his own hands and offered sacrifice, and swung the censer, thereby trampling on the command of God and assuming to be the supreme religious ruler of the world and to make a worship according to his own plan. And later on he made a foolish law, on a battlefield, that if anyone should eat any food on that day he should be killed. His own son, Jonathan, in a distant part of the field, did not know of that command and ate some honey, and King Saul was going to have his own son slain in order to carry out a foolish and devilish law which he had made against all reason; but the people hindered him from his insane act. This proves that King Saul, before he died, had in him the propensity to institute a religion full of murder and cruelty, and shows us how easy it will be for him to be the tool of the devil in forming the person of the Antichrist and usurping all of the religious rights and dictating all worship.

In the sixth place, the Antichrist will be the special foe of the true Christ, the Lamb of God and will seek to antagonize the Lord Jesus Christ at every single point and with the utmost malice. This is exactly what King Saul did in his bitter persecution against David, the true king chosen of God. He sought in every way, for over fifteen years, to slay David. So in this respect Saul and the Antichrist agree exactly.

In the seventh place, the Antichrist will be a man slain by the sword before he goes down into the abyss. The prophet Isaiah gives us a picture of the Antichrist under the type of the king of Babylon, and speaks of him as having a more terrible death than the kings of the nations, and says: "Thou art cast out of thy grave like an abominable branch, and as the raiment of those that are slain, thrust through with a sword, that go down to the stones of the pit" (Isaiah 14:19).

We also read in Zech. 11:17, "Woe to the idol shepherd (that is, the shepherd that claims to be worshiped) for the sword shall be upon his arm and upon his right eye, and his arm shall be clean dried up, and his right eye shall be utterly darkened." Again, we read in Rev. 13:10, "He that leadeth into captivity shall go into captivity, and he that killeth with the sword must be killed with the sword." The Antichrist will at first capture the world, but Jesus and the white horse army of saints will capture him, and he who killed so many by the sword must himself die by the sword. It is in agreement with these Scriptures that King Saul fell upon his own sword and slew himself (1 Sam. 31:4).

The Antichrist dies by the sword, but the false prophet dies by hanging himself. For example, Absalom was a type of the Antichrist, and he was slain by the sword in the hand of Joab; but Ahithophel, his great counselor, was a type of the false prophet, and he died by hanging himself. And the same words are used in Scripture both of Ahithophel and of Judas Iscariot.

Now, put all these points together and consider that King Saul is the only man that has ever lived in the world in whom all these points agree both with him and with the Antichrist, and to my mind it is perfectly clear that Saul will be resurrected in the judgment time and will be the Antichrist. Just as God the Father gives all his estate to his Son, Jesus Christ, so we are told that the dragon – that is, Satan – will give all his power to the Antichrist.

At the time when the Lord Jesus and the glorified saints come riding down on their white horses, this great Antichrist will be seeking to kill all the Jews in the world because they still adhere to the teaching that there is one true God, and because they have revolted from the Antichrist's dominion; and in that awful crisis, just before the Antichrist succeeds in killing the Jews, they will be delivered by the glorious apocalypse of the Lord Jesus, revealed in flaming fire with his angels and glorified saints, and at that time the Antichrist and his false prophet will be seized and cast alive into the lake of fire, according to Rev. 19:20. This will be the destruction spoken of by Paul in Thessalonians.

The very fact that the Antichrist and the false prophet are cast alive into the lake of fire goes to show that they had both previously died and come up from the abyss, because every sinner in the world must die before passing into his eternal destiny.

You notice that all the armies of the Antichrist are slain with the sword that proceeds from the mouth of Christ, but the beast and the false prophet are not slain in that way; they are cast alive into burning brimstone, thus marking the difference between those two characters and the great army of sinners that fight under them.

That event will remove from the earth every form of organized wickedness and every form of human government, and be the glorious consummation for which the righteous have prayed all through human history.

This destruction of the Antichrist does not imply his annihilation, for we are told in chapter 20 that after the thousand-year reign, those two men, the beast and the false prophet, are still existing in the lake of fire after having been there a thousand years. So there is no such teaching as that of annihilation for the wicked; and destruction, in the Bible sense of that word, does not imply annihilation, but the complete undoing and wrecking of one's life and destiny.

CHAPTER 17

The Chaining of Satan

THE last hindrance to be removed before the setting up of Christ's kingdom on earth is that of the chaining of Satan, and with him all the demons who are under his authority, into the abyss, and this clears the way for Christ and the glorified saints to establish their dominion over the whole earth, and over all those nations or peoples who have not been destroyed during the great tribulation. This event follows immediately after the destruction of the Antichrist and the slaying of all the armies that fought under him. "And I saw an angel come down from heaven having the key of the bottomless pit and a great chain in his hand, and he laid hold on the dragon, that old serpent, which is the devil and Satan, and bound him a thousand years, and cast him into the bottomless pit, and shut him up, and set a seal upon him, that he should deceive the nations no more till the thousand years should be fulfilled, and after that he must be loosed a little season" (Rev. 20:1-3).

As Satan was the first agent of evil, that tempted our first parents in the Garden of Eden, and sowed the seed of all the corruption and woe in the history of the human race, so he is the last one to be removed from the surface of the earth and from having any power over human beings living in the flesh. Satan was the great agent behind all the former battles in human history, and behind all the history of the mother of harlots and Babylon and the Antichrist and all other forces of evil. Satan will see the complete overthrow of all his kingdom and his devices to wreck and ruin the human race, and after he has seen his greatest production, in the Antichrist, go down into the lake of fire, then he himself will be seized and shut up in the abyss. In order to grasp the full import of this passage on the chaining of Satan, let us note the following points:

1. Four different names are given to the devil in this Scripture-that is, "the dragon," "the old serpent," "the devil," and "Satan." These are all of the names given to Satan in the Bible, and these four names perfectly set forth his character and various functions as manifested in the history of the world.

We can always find a revelation of divine truth in studying the different names that God gives to persons, places or things in the Scriptures. Names are not accidental with God, but are always given and used with special significance, and this is as true with the names of Satan as it is with the different names that are given to Christ or to his servants.

The name "dragon" is given to Satan in reference to politics and earthly sovereignty. It is from the dragon that rises out of the abyss, or that comes down from the air, or that makes war with Michael for the supremacy of the government of this world. For long centuries the dragon was the emblem of the Chinese government on their flags, and it was Satan himself that led the Chinese rulers in ages past to put the dragon on their flags.

There are several Scriptures in which Satan claims authority over all kingdoms of the world, and he proposed to give these kingdoms to Christ if He would bow down and worship him.

The name of "the old serpent" is always given in reference to deceit, temptation, and treachery, in any attempt to seduce the servants of God, and tempt the righteous into ways of disobedience. It was the "serpent" that tempted Eve to eat the forbidden fruit, and not the dragon, or the devil, or Satan; but emphatically the serpent, because that name belongs to him whenever he attempts to tempt the righteous. The apostle Paul refers to this same name in one of his epistles, in which he urges the Gentile converts to beware of the tempter, lest the old *serpent* that tempted Eve should also tempt those who were espoused to be the bride of Christ; and he calls the devil by that name, "serpent."

The name "devil" is always applied in reference to his true character as a liar and a murderer. The deepest part of the devil's character is that of a murderer and a liar, and Scripture says that the devil is a liar and the father of lies, and also it is said he was a murderer from the beginning.

The name "Satan" is always given in reference to being an adversary, like a tricky, shrewd lawyer, one who brings false accusations and trumps up false and slanderous arguments. Hence we read that it was Satan that accused Job to the Lord. And in the book of Zechariah, it is Satan that stands up to bring false charges against the priest of the Lord.

These four names embrace every part of the character of Satan, and also set forth every variety of his iniquity and wicked conduct. The personality of the devil is revealed in Scripture as positively as the personality of God or of any angel or of any man. The delusion in modern heresy that Satan is only a principle or a kind of a law is itself the effect of Satan's teaching, for it is his policy to delude the human race and make them ignore his personality and his agency and to deny his character and his work.

2. Let us notice this mighty angel that comes down from heaven having the key of the abyss – for that is the word which is translated "bottomless pit." I am very sure that this angel is the angel Jehovah, the Lord Jesus himself, who is so often referred to in the book of Revelation as an angel, or as "another angel," and there are a great many actions which are affirmed of this angel that no mere creature could perform. It is the Jehovah angel, incarnate as the Son of man that is the seed of the woman that is to bruise Satan's head. We are told that when Michael the archangel had a contest with Satan over the dead body of Moses, the archangel did not bring a railing accusation against Satan, but said, "The Lord rebuke thee," showing that it was the Lord; that is, Jehovah, who was the proper one to rebuke Satan. The devil wanted to show the Israelites where the dead body of Moses was buried in order that he might induce them to worship that body, and the archangel Michael was sent to withstand Satan and prevent the people from finding the dead body of Moses, and thereby deliver them from idolatry. It was a hot contest of words and arguments and strategy, and the contest did not terminate

until Satan was rebuked by Jehovah the Lord Jesus. It is Christ who says: "I have the keys of death and of hell," or, more properly the keys of death and Hades; that is, the keys of the grave where the body is buried, and the key of Hades where the departed spirit goes down in the under part of the earth. These Scripture references and many others that might be referred to prove conclusively that this great angel that had the keys of the abyss was none other person than the Lord Jesus, the supreme conqueror of the devil and the one who has authority to chain or to loose, to open or to shut, which none can hinder.

3. Let us notice the great chain with which Satan is to be bound. In the very nature of things, this chain is to be a real, literal chain, of a nature sufficient to bind the fallen angel. So many Bible readers ask the question, How can a chain bind a spirit? But this Scripture does not say anything about an iron chain, and it is useless to put in that word "iron" in reference to this act of chaining. There is a spirit world as absolutely as there is a material world, and God can make a spirit chain as easily as men make an iron chain, and God can chain a spirit just as effectually as men can chain an animal with a material chain.

The apostle Jude tells us that there are certain fallen angels who did not keep their first estate, and that they are at the present time reserved in chains under darkness until the time of the great judgment. There are different ranks of demons, for the Scriptures abundantly teach us that there are countless numbers of demons that are loose in the world, and that operate upon human beings and upon the elements of nature; and then there are other demons who are so terrific that God will not let them loose at the present time, and they are bound in chains until the judgment. They are the demons that are to be let loose in the great tribulation judgment as described in Revelation 9, and who have the form of locusts, and they will torment the ungodly in the tribulation judgment. Now, if these demons are at present bound in chains, it is most certain that Christ can bind Satan with the same kind of chain. We ourselves possess a spirit nature; in fact, our personality resides in our human spirit, and yet we know that this spirit which constitutes our own personality is at the present time chained in our human bodies, and we have no power to separate our souls or our spirits from our bodies except by death. And hence how foolish it is for anyone to suppose that the omnipotent Son of God cannot chain Satan with a spirit chain perfectly effectual in confining the devil to any part of creation which God may choose.

4. Let us notice the locality where Satan is placed. It is called in our English the "bottomless pit," and the Greek word is "abyss," which signifies the hollow place at the center of our earth. The Bible reveals various localities inside of this world, and there is nothing in science or the knowledge of material creation that can disprove such statements.

The Hebrew Scriptures speak of an upper Hades and a lower Hades, and between these two localities a great gulf is fixed across which no one can pass. According to the Old Testament the souls of the righteous dead were kept in the upper Hades, and the souls of the wicked dead were confined in the lower Hades, and David said that when God saved him he delivered his soul from the lower Hades. Our English Bible reads, "the lowest Hades," but literally it is the *lower Hades.* When Jesus arose from the dead, we are told in two places in Scripture that he took the souls of the righteous dead from the lower parts of the earth up into heaven, or into paradise, so that since the ascension of Christ, when the righteous die their souls ascend into Paradise and do not descend into Hades, but the wicked dead souls are still reserved in Hades awaiting the final judgment.

But this place which is called the abyss is not Hades. It is an empty space in the center of the earth, and according to Scripture there are only two human beings that ever go down into the abyss: one is the man who is to be the Antichrist, and the other is the man who is to be the false prophet, who, very likely, are King Saul and Judas Iscariot; and both of these are said to come up from the abyss in the judgment time. Now, that is the place where Satan is to be confined with all his demons during the thousand-year reign of Christ and the saints upon this earth.

5. Notice some features connected with the chaining of Satan: It is instantaneous, by one supreme act of the almighty Son of God, and not a slow, gradual process of weakening the devil's power on the earth. Every word in this passage referring to the chaining of Satan is, in the Greek, in the aorist tense, which always signifies an instantaneous act and not a gradual process. In the passage above quoted the following words are all in the aorist tense: "laid hold," "bound," "cast," "shut up," "set a seal." All these words indicate an instantaneous act of the personal Lord Jesus, and not a slow process of reducing the devil's power by the church or by the gospel. It is amazing how a foolish prejudice in the minds of great scholars will make them stultify their own common sense in the study or the translation of Bible words.

Some years ago an eminent Greek scholar wrote an article on instantaneous sanctification, and he proved from the Greek Testament that the verbs which refer to sanctification were always in the aorist tense, to prove an instantaneous heart cleansing in contrast to the slow process of gradual growth. That same scholar was furiously opposed to any teaching on the pre-millennial coming of Christ, and when someone asked him what the Scripture on the chaining of the devil meant, he wrote an article saying that the chaining of the devil was a slow, gradual process of curtailing satanic power, and that every time there was a religious revival or a new church built, or a new mission field opened up, it was the gradual limiting of satanic power, and that is what was meant by the chaining of Satan. That great scholar stultified his own common sense and all his Greek scholarship by refusing to admit that all these words referring to the chaining of Satan were in the aorist tense, just as perfectly as were the verbs on instantaneous sanctification. Countless millions of churches and millions of revivals could never have any power to chain the devil, for there is only one person in the universe that can chain him, and that is the Son of God. That great event will come to pass at the end of this age and just before the opening of the kingdom age. Where our English Bible reads that the devil is the god of this world, it should be rendered he is the god of this age, and when this age closes Satan will no longer be the god of this age, but he will be chained and locked up in the abyss. And this poor world will have a rest from his dominion, agency and power. Satan is still loose, and according to Scripture he is at the present time the prince of the powers of the air, and he rules in the hearts of the disobedient sons of men.

6. In this connection, let us notice the four stages to the downfall and doom of the devil. His first fall was from his place as an archangel in the glorious presence of God, down into the character of a liar and a murderer, and he fell from the upper heaven of God's glory down into the heaven which properly belongs to this earth. When the word "heaven" in the original refers to the upper heavens, the word is in the plural number, as where it says, "Our Father who art in the heavens," – plural. But where the word "heaven" applies locally to the blue sky and the upper regions of the air, the upper heavens that belong to this earth, the original word is in the singular number and prefixed by the article "the," – "the heaven." For instance, Rev. 12:1, "There appeared a great sign in the heaven," that is, in the local heaven that belongs to this earth, and so of all other similar Scriptures.

The second stage in the fall of Satan will take place during the great tribulation as described in Revelation 12, where the archangel Michael will fight with the dragon up in the heaven – that is, our local heaven above this earth; and he will be cast down upon the earth and lose his place from the sky, and hence of the powers of the air, and be limited to move on the surface of the earth, which will be an awful humiliation to his satanic pride in those judgment times. It is for this reason that he becomes enraged against Israel and has great wrath, because he knows he will then have but a short time before he is chained in the abyss. Hence we see that in chapter 13, the devil raises the great Antichrist and imparts all his power to the Antichrist, which is the consummation and climax of all satanic wrath and achievement in this world.

The next stage in the downfall of Satan is where he will be chained and shut up in the abyss with all his demons, to stay there a thousand years, with no power to reach a single person on the face of the earth.

The fourth and last stage of the devil's downfall is at the close of the thousand-year reign, when he will be loosed again for a short while in order to sift out the hypocrites which have lived through the millennial age, and then he is seized and judged and cast into the lake of fire and brimstone, where the beast, that is, Antichrist, and the false prophet have been kept for a thousand years, and where they still are. The devil is from thenceforth confined to the lake of fire, to be tormented day and night forever and ever (Rev. 20: 10). This is the last time that Satan is mentioned in the Bible.

How perfectly the Word of God furnishes us with the description and history of the devil from the beginning to the ending of this world – of his first appearance as a serpent to tempt our first parents, on through all the history of the human race, until finally he is cast into the lake of fire, to remain there forever and ever.

The carnal mind is the special work of the devil in the human heart, and there is a perfect agreement between Satan and the carnal mind. The carnal mind will always act just like Satan under similar circumstances. Just as Satan is bound, and after that is cast into the lake of fire, so Jesus teaches that the strong man, the old man, the carnal mind, is first bound and then cast out and his goods destroyed. There is a close analogy between the work of Satan in this world and the work of a carnal mind in a human being, but God has made provision for the complete removal of the carnal mind from the soul, and the utter and final removal of Satan from this world.

CHAPTER 8

The Kingdom Age

IN this series of Bible expositions, we have traced the progress of the redeemed children of the Lord from their calling out of Egypt, that is, their conversion, on through the different stages of Christian progress, through death or translation, and come to the events that will transpire while they are up in heaven with Christ, and then their return riding on white horses to destroy the Antichrist and to witness the chaining of Satan; and now we have come to the age of the kingdom, or the thousand-year reign which is spoken of in Rev. 20:4-6. "And I saw thrones, and they (that is, the resurrected saints) sat upon them, and judgment (that is, power to judge or to govern) was given unto them: and I saw the souls of them that were beheaded for the witness of Jesus, and for the word of God, and which had not worshiped the beast (or the Antichrist), neither his image, neither had received his mark upon their foreheads, or in their hands: and they lived (that is, lived again) and reigned with Christ a thousand years. But the rest of the dead (that is, the wicked dead) lived not again until the thousand years were finished. This is the first resurrection. Blessed and holy is he that hath part in the first resurrection: on such the second death hath no power, but they shall be priests of God and of Christ, and shall reign with him a thousand years."

This is the final statement regarding what we call the millennium, or the thousand-year reign which the glorified saints are to have over this world. There are a great many Scriptures referring to this kingdom age scattered all through the Bible, from the writings of Moses, through all prophecy, and in the gospels and in the epistles; but in this passage we have the final statement and fulfillment of those Scriptures.

During the first age, from Adam to the flood, there was no law, no church, no Bible; but the human race was governed by their conscience, acted on by the Holy Spirit. In the Mosaic, or Jewish age, they not only had the conscience but in addition they had the law, both the moral and the ceremonial law, and the prophets, with all the types concerning redemption. The age of law closed with the crucifixion of Jesus, and on the day of Pentecost there was opened up the church or gospel age, in which the people not only had the conscience and the law – that is, moral law – but they had the Holy Ghost, the Christian church with its ordinances and sacraments and gospel ministry. The church age will close with the rapture, when Christ gathers his people to himself up in the sky and institutes the judgment on the living nations. The kingdom age will begin when Christ with his glorified saints returns, riding down from the marriage supper. And when Satan is chained, then the glorified Jesus with the resurrected saints will take charge of this entire world; and the Messianic throne, according to many Scriptures, will be set up in Jerusalem, which will be rebuilt, according to Isaiah, with precious stones of sapphires and carbuncles and agates, and then will the kingdom come for which the people have been sighing and praying for six thousand years.

The kingdom will be like the King. Christ was not of the earth, but he came down from heaven to earth; and so the kingdom of God is not of this world; that is, not out from the world, but, like the King, it will come down from heaven and be established upon the earth.

There are a great many things spoken of in Scripture in connection with this kingdom age, and I shall have to condense my remarks upon this subject, as I wish to set forth many of the Scriptures on this subject.

1. No one but regenerated people will be able to see this kingdom. Jesus says: "Except a man be born again he cannot see the kingdom of God." He does not say that the new birth is essential in order to see the church, because millions of unconverted people have seen the church; but there is a great difference

between the church and the kingdom, and no one can see the kingdom except they who have been born the second time from above and changed by the Holy Spirit. A perfect illustration of this is furnished in the resurrection of Christ. Sinners saw Jesus during his lifetime, and they saw him dead on the cross. But after he was buried, no sinner ever saw him after that. And when he was resurrected we are distinctly told in Scripture that no one saw him except chosen witnesses, and all who gazed on his glorified humanity were those who had been born of God and were qualified to be witnesses of his resurrection. This is a perfect sample of the fact that sinners can see the church, while the church is in this age, but when the church shall pass into the translation, or the resurrection, and be merged into the kingdom age, then no sinner will see it. Before the kingdom is set up, all sinners and rebellious persons will be killed or die in the great tribulation judgment, and only those will be spared to pass into the millennium who submit to Jesus and become regenerated. According to Zechariah, two-thirds of the human race will die in the tribulation judgment, and the other one-third will submit themselves to the Lord and be spared to pass into the millennium, and they will constitute the living nations on the earth, that will multiply so enormously in the thousand-year reign.

2. We must remember that all who have been resurrected and glorified will live in glorified bodies through the kingdom age with their home up in the air, having perfect control of their bodies to manifest themselves at will, to transport themselves through the air to any point on the earth, and manifest themselves to the people on the earth at will, just exactly as Jesus did in the forty days after his resurrection. The manner in which Christ existed during the forty days after his resurrection was a perfect sample of the way in which the glorified saints are to live through the thousand-year reign. But those nations that are living on the earth and that submit themselves to God in the tribulation judgment, and are spared to live through the thousand-year reign, their bodies will not be glorified, but their lives will be lengthened out like it was before the flood. Saint Paul

speaks of bodies that are terrestrial and bodies that are celestial, and hence the nations on the earth will live in their terrestrial bodies, but the glorified saints will live in celestial bodies.

3. We must remember that the changes which will take place in the kingdom age over the church age will be far greater than the changes in any previous ages. There were wonderful changes that took place after the close of the conscience age, as, for instance, human life was cut short, and the human race was allowed to eat meat, which had not been the case before the flood: and a great many changes took place in the laws of nature as well as in the human constitution. And then there were great changes that took place after the close of the Jewish age, such as the doing away with the ceremonial law and animal sacrifices, and the institution of the gospel ministry, and the church sacraments, and worldwide evangelism, and these were marvelous changes from the old order of the Mosaic institutions.

Now, at the close of the church age, when the kingdom age has come, there will be still greater changes throughout the realm of nature and in the constitution of animals and the four seasons as well as in the dominion established over the earth. There will be an end to the church age, to the gospel ministry, to the Christian sacraments, and an end to all mere human education as well as great changes in the systems of nature. According to Scripture, the curse will be lifted from the lower creation. The apostle Paul tells us that the lower creation shall be delivered from the bondage of corruption and enter into the glorious liberty of the children of God, and that the present groaning of the whole creation will pass away at the time of the redemption of our human bodies (Romans 8:21-23). In fact, the kingdom age will be the great fulfillment of the jubilee of the world, of which the institution of the jubilee year in the Mosaic law was a prophetic type, in which all debts were canceled, and all estates that had been mortgaged were restored to the original owners, and all wrongs were righted.

4. The center of the Messianic government will be located in Jerusalem. "At that time they shall call Jerusalem the throne of the Lord; and all the nations shall be gathered unto it, to the

name of the Lord, to Jerusalem: neither shall they walk any more after the imagination of their evil heart" (Jer. 3:17). This word has never yet been fulfilled, and the only time in which it can be fulfilled is during the kingdom age which is yet to come.

"Of the increase of his government and peace there shall be no end, upon the throne of David, and upon his kingdom, to order it, and to establish it with judgment and with justice from henceforth even forever. The zeal of the Lord of hosts will perform this" (Isaiah 9:7). The throne of David most certainly is not the throne of the eternal Father up in the heavens, but the Messianic throne which was founded in king David, and is to be restored and perpetuated and in the Lord Jesus who is descended from David, and who is to sit on David's throne; and that throne was in Jerusalem.

"Behold, the days come, saith the Lord, when I will raise unto David a righteous Branch, and a King shall reign and prosper, and shall execute judgment and justice in the earth" (Jer. 23:5). You see, this prophecy does not refer to the throne of God in heaven, but most positively to the throne of David, and the execution of judgment and justice in the earth. And it can only mean what it says.

"And in the days of these kings shall the God of heaven set up a kingdom, which shall never be destroyed: and the kingdom shall not be left to other people, but it shall break in pieces and consume all these kingdoms, and it shall stand for ever" (Daniel 2 :44). This proves that the kingdom that God will set up is to occupy the very same territory that the kingdoms of the world occupied, so that the locality of God's kingdom on earth is fixed by this fact, that it covers the same countries that the four worldwide kingdoms occupied.

"But the saints of the Most High shall take the kingdom, and possess the kingdom for ever, even for ever and ever. And the kingdom and dominion, and the greatness of the kingdom under the whole heaven, shall be given to the people of the saints of the Most High, whose kingdom is an everlasting kingdom, and all dominions shall serve and obey him" (Daniel 7:18 and 27). Here we notice it is expressly stated that the kingdom is not to be up in heaven, but located under the whole heaven, that is, over this earth; and this kingdom, we are told in the same chapter, is to take the place of the four great kingdoms that had previously been on the earth.

"And the Lord shall be king over all the earth: in that day shall there be one Lord, and his name one. And men shall dwell in it, and there shall be no more utter destruction; but Jerusalem shall be safely inhabited. In that day shall there be upon the bells of the horses, HOLINESS UNTO THE LORD; and the pots in the Lord's house shall be like the bowls before the altar. Yea, every pot in Jerusalem and in Judah shall be holiness unto the Lord" (Zech. 14).

5. The glorified saints will be partakers with Christ in ruling and judging the world in that kingdom age. "And Peter said, Behold, we have forsaken all, and followed thee; what shall we have therefore? And Jesus said unto them, Verily I say unto you, that ye which have followed me, in the regeneration (the Greek word is *palegenesis,* which means the universal regeneration of the saved ones) when the Son of man shall sit in the throne of his glory, ye shall also sit upon twelve thrones, judging the twelve tribes of Israel (Matt. 19:27-28).

"He that overcometh, and keepeth my works unto the end, to him will I give power (or authority) over the nations: and he shall rule them (or literally, *shepherdize them*) with a rod of iron; as the vessels of a potter shall they be broken to shivers: even as I received of my Father" (Rev. 2:26-27). "To him that overcometh will I grant to sit with me in my throne, even as I also overcame, and am set down with my Father in his throne" (Rev. 3:21).

All these Scriptures are very specific, and show that the glorified saints are to have thrones in fellowship with the King, and share with Christ in his authority over the nations, and that all the world will be divided into provinces and subdivisions, and put under the glorified saints, who will have charge of all the affairs of the human race as to education, arts, industries, teaching, training, correcting, and settling up all matters whether of business or of religion, and be the teachers of spiritual truth to all the inhabited earth. This is expressed in the song of the glorified saints where they sing, "Unto him that loved us, and washed us from our sins in his own blood, and hath made us kings and priests (or, more literally, a kingdom of priests) unto God and his Father; to him be glory and dominion for ever and ever, Amen" (Rev. 1:5-6).

David tells us, in the forty-ninth Psalm, that the upright are going to have dominion over the world in the morning, that is, in the great resurrection morning.

Paul says, "If we suffer with Christ, we shall also reign with Him." We are now living in the suffering age, but we shall then live in the reigning age. He will give grace and glory. Grace in this age, and glory in the kingdom age. Paul says that the kingdom will appear when Christ appears, at his appearing and kingdom. (2 Tim. 4:1). The cross is the explanation of everything in the church age, and the throne is the explanation of everything in the kingdom age.

6. The earth is to be filled with the knowledge and glory of God in the kingdom age. "But as truly as I live, all the earth shall be filled with the glory of the Lord" (Num. 14:21). Those words were given to Moses at the time that the people of Israel refused to enter Canaan at Kadesh-barnea, and were turned back to tarry in the wilderness, and which may be regarded as the darkest days in the life of Moses; yet, at that very time, God prophesied the coming of the kingdom age, when the earth should be full of glory.

"He maketh wars to cease unto the end of the earth; he breaketh the bow, and cutteth the spear in sunder; he burneth the chariot in the fire. Be still, and know that I am God: I will be exalted among the heathen, I will be exalted in the earth" (Psa. 46:9-10). There never will be a cessation of wars until God brings it to pass at the close of the great tribulation, and then he will destroy every instrument of battle, and put a divine stillness over the whole earth; and the Lord Jesus will be exalted in the earth, and perfect peace and quietness will fill the world.

"Let the nations be glad and sing for joy: for thou shalt judge the people righteously, and govern the nations upon earth. Let the people praise thee, O God; let all the people praise thee. Then shall the earth yield her increase; and God, even our own God, shall bless us: and all the ends of the earth shall fear him" (Psa. 67:4-7).

Here is a prophecy not only of the earth being full of God's glory, but also that the earth will yield her increase. When God put the curse on Adam, he also cursed the ground on man's account, and from that time the earth has never yielded a full crop, and it is by toil and sweat that man gets a scanty harvest. But when the kingdom has come, the curse will be lifted; the earth will then yield abundantly, and likely one acre of land will be sufficient to support a large family.

The entire seventy second Psalm is a prophecy of the glorious time of the kingdom age, when Jehovah, the Lord Jesus, shall judge the people in righteousness, and all nations shall fear him, and he will come down like the rain upon mown grass, and the righteous shall flourish, and the lives of the people shall be precious in his sight. That Psalm was entitled, "A Prayer for Solomon," but really it is for Solomon's greater Son, the Messiah. And in that prayer David had a vision of the kingdom time, and closed the prayer by saying, "Blessed be the Lord God, the God of Israel, who only doeth wondrous things. And blessed be his glorious name for ever: and let the whole earth be filled with his glory: Amen, and Amen. The prayers of David the son of Jesse are ended." The proper translation of the last clause should be, The prayers of David the son of Jesse *have reached their perfect fulfillment;* that is, when Christ shall reign on earth; and when the words of that psalm are all fulfilled, that will be the ultimate answer of all David's prayers.

"Mercy and truth are met together; righteousness and peace have kissed each other. Truth shall spring out of the earth; and righteousness shall look down from heaven. Yea, the Lord shall give that which is good; and our land shall yield her increase" (Psa. 85:10-12). In this present age the earth often deceives us and blights the seed and gives thorns and briars and weeds instead of grain; and the heavens often deceive us with late frosts or early storms before the harvest is gathered: but in the kingdom age the heaven and the earth will be under the most perfect regulation as to climatic conditions, and there will be no disappointment in sowing seed or reaping the harvests, but every element of nature will work in perfect order and regularity without any damage.

"Sing unto the Lord with the harp, and the voice of a psalm. With trumpets and sound of cornet make a joyful noise before the Lord, the King. Let the sea roar, and the fullness thereof: the world, and they that dwell therein. Let the floods clap their hands: let the hills be joyful together before the Lord: for he cometh to judge the earth: with righteousness shall he judge the world, and the people with equity" (Psa. 98:5-9). Those words will have fulfillment only in the kingdom age.

"It shall come to pass in the last days, that the mountain of the Lord's house shall be established in the top of the mountains, and shall be exalted above the hills; and all na? tions shall flow unto it. And many people shall go and say, Come ye, and let us go up to the mountain of the Lord, to the house of the God of Jacob; and he will teach us of his ways, and we will walk in his paths: for out of Zion shall go forth the law, and the word of the Lord from Jerusalem. And he shall judge among the nations, and shall rebuke many people: and they shall beat their swords into plow-shares, and their spears into pruning hooks: nation shall not lift up sword against nation, neither shall they learn war any more" (Isaiah 2:2-4). Those words have never yet been fulfilled, but will be literally accomplished in the coming kingdom.

"With righteousness shall the Lord judge the poor, and reprove with equity for the meek of the earth. And righteousness shall be the girdle of his loins. The wolf also shall dwell with the lamb, and the leopard shall lie down with the kid; and the calf and the young lion and the fatling together; and a little child shall lead them. And the cow and the bear shall feed; their young ones shall lie down together; and the lion shall eat straw like the ox. They shall not hurt nor destroy in all my holy mountain: for the earth shall be full of the knowledge of the Lord, as the waters cover the sea" (Isaiah 11:4-9). In the present age, lions and other wild beasts live on flesh; but in the coming age their natures will be changed so that they will have no taste for flesh, but live on grass like the oxen. It would seem from Scripture that no wild beast ever lived on flesh before the flood; and that the human race did not eat meat before the flood; but that at the time of the flood the constitution of men and animals changed so that they needed meat. But in the kingdom age the constitution of the animal will be put back where it was originally, so that all the animals will live on grass, and the human race will live on fruit and grains, without any need of meat.

"In mercy shall the throne be established: and he shall sit upon it in truth in the tabernacle of David, judging, and seeking judgment, and hasting righteousness. And then the outcasts will dwell in safety, and Jehovah will be a covert for them; and the extortioner and the spoiler and the oppressor shall be consumed out of the land" (Isaiah 16:4-5). Here is another proof that the Messiah will occupy the throne of David and be the preserver of perfect peace to all the people on the earth.

"And in this mountain shall the Lord of hosts make unto all people a feast of fat things, a feast of wines on the lees, of fat things full of marrow, of wine on the lea well refined. And he will destroy in this mountain the face of the covering cast over all people, and the vail that is spread over all nations. He will swallow up death in victory; and the Lord God will wipe away tears from off all faces; and the rebuke of his people shall he take away from off all the earth; for the Lord hath spoken it" (Isaiah 25:6-8). We are now living in a time when there is a veil over all human minds, and people do not see eye to eye; but in the resurrection state, when Jesus reigns, the veil will be taken from all eyes and we shall see eye to eye when the Lord bringeth again Zion.

"For thou shalt be in league with the stones of the field: and the beasts of the field shall be at peace with thee. At destruction and famine thou shalt laugh: neither shalt thou be afraid of the beasts of the earth. And thou shalt know that thy tabernacle shall be in peace; and thou shalt visit thy habitation, and shalt not sin, and thine offspring shall be as the grass of the earth" (Job 5:22-25). This is one among many Scriptures showing that in the kingdom age there will be no danger from the animals or from bad climates, but that the nations on the earth will be in harmony with God and all the laws of nature in harmony with the best welfare of mankind.

"Behold the days come, saith the Lord, that the plowman shall overtake the reaper, and the treader of grapes him that soweth seed; and the mountains shall drop sweet wine, and all the hills shall melt. And I will bring again the captivity of my people of Israel, and they shall build the waste cities, and inhabit them; and they shall plant vineyards, and drink the wine thereof; they shall also make gardens, and eat the fruit of them. And I will plant them upon their land, and they shall no more be pulled up out of their land which I have given them, saith the Lord thy God" (Amos 9: 13-15). It is in the kingdom age that Israel is to be restored to their own land, and be put at the head of all the nations of the earth, according to many passages in the Word. We notice in this passage that the harvests will be so abundant that it will be time to plow and plant before the reaper has succeeded in removing the old crop from the fields.

"There shall be no more thence an infant of days, nor an old man that hath not filled his days: for the child shall die an hundred years old; but the sinner being an hundred years old shall be accursed. And they shall build houses and inhabit them: and they shall plant vineyards, and eat the fruit of them. They shall not build, and another inhabit; they shall not plant, and another eat: for as the days of a tree are the days of my people, and mine elect shall long enjoy the work of their hands. They shall not labor in vain, nor bring forth for trouble; for they are the seed of the blessed of the Lord, and their offspring with them. The wolf and the lamb shall feed together, and the lion shall eat straw like the bullock. They shall not hurt nor destroy in all my holy mountain, saith the Lord" (Isaiah 65:20-25). This prophecy does not refer to the glorified saints, but to the nations living on the earth, and especially to the Israelites who will then be restored to their own land. The expression, "They shall not bring forth for trouble," is a distinct prophecy that God will remove the pangs of child-birth from the mothers in the kingdom age, and also the passages teaches perfect healthfulness, the absence of deformity, such as blindness, lameness, deafness, and the many afflictions which so many have to endure in the present age. Under those perfect regulations of life and health, the human race will multiply by billions, and all the waste places of the earth will be inhabited. The deserts, as we are told elsewhere, will blossom like the rose, for the barren lands will be irrigated and the whole earth will be like the garden of the Lord.

Trees of certain varieties live a thousand years, and we have trees in California that are four and five thousand years old; and the promise is, that the nations who live in the millennium will live like these trees, for many centuries, or until the close of the thousand-year reign, when all the righteous ones will pass into their glorified state.

"In that day shall the Lord defend the inhabitants of Jeru-salem; and he that is feeble among them at that day shall be as David; and the house of David shall be as God, as the angel of the Lord before them" (Zech. 12:8). Here we see that the people will be so much stronger in the kingdom age than they are now, for there will be advancement on every line. Those who are weak in the present age, if they were living in the kingdom age would be strong as giants, and those who are strong in the present life, were they living in the millennium, would be like angels in their vigor. It is impossible for us to imagine the infinite changes that will take place at that time, and the countless advantages that will come to the world in that age. We often speak of the inventions and advantages of the present day over those of ancient times, long past, and yet the progress of advantages in the millennial age will be far beyond any dreams we can have in the present state of our existence.

We are told in another place that in those days the light of the moon will be as bright as the light of the sun is now, and that the light of the sun will be seven times brighter than at the present time. Thus all the elements of sunlight and moonlight, the seasons, the climates, the nature of animals, the health and vigor of the human body and everything that relates to the welfare of the human race, will be marvelously advanced over the present condition of things.

We are also told in prophecy that at that time God will restore to the human race a pure language, which implies that all nations in the world will speak one language, which will perfectly simplify the matter of education and of communication between the various peoples.

There are not less than fifty places in the Bible which prophesy the things that will take place in the kingdom age, and these various prophecies cover the entire range of everything in nature and humanity, in government, in prosperity, in health, as well as in righteousness among the people and in the manifestation of the glory of God to all the nations that will live on the earth.

CHAPTER 19

The New Jerusalem

"AND I saw a new heaven and a new earth; and I saw the holy city, new Jerusalem, coming down from God out of heaven, prepared as a bride adorned for her husband. And I heard a great voice saying, Behold, the tabernacle of God is with men, and he will dwell with them and they shall be his people. And God shall wipe all tears from their eyes; and there shall be no more death, neither sorrow, nor crying, for the former things are passed away. And one of the seven angels talked with me, saying, Come hither, I will show thee the bride, the Lamb's wife. And he carried me away in the spirit to a great and high mountain, and showed me that great city, the holy Jerusalem, descending out of heaven like unto a stone most precious, even like a jasper stone, clear as crystal. And the city was pure gold, like unto clear glass" (Rev. 21).

This city is the last of all the revelations that God has made to men in his Word.

The first Jerusalem was built on the earth; the second Jerusalem is built somewhere up in the heavens. The first was built of stone; the second is built of pure gold. The first was built by man, probably Melchizedek at its first beginning, but the second is built by God himself. The first was the center of government for God's earthly people; the second is the center of government for all worlds and all ages. The first had in it the throne of David and was the center of the theocratic kingdom of Israel; the second has in it the throne of God and of the Lamb, and is the center of all spiritual empire and authority. The first was for a kingdom on the earth, for men living in the flesh; the second is for the kingdom of heaven, and inhabited by glorified and redeemed humanity. The first is where the Lamb of God was crucified for the sins of the world; the second is where the Lamb is in the midst of the throne, the glorified Redeemer, the King of kings, the Lord of lords. The first had in it a pool of water called Siloam; the second has in it a river of pure water, clear as crystal, proceeding out of the throne of God and the Lamb. The first, when in a fallen condition, was compared by Saint Paul to Hagar, the bondmaid, who was in bondage with her children; the second is compared to Sarah, the mother of Israel and the typical mother of all saints, the free woman, the wife of the Lamb. The first is referred to as a city that can be shaken, by Paul in Hebrews, and that will be shaken in the end; but the second is referred to as a city which cannot be shaken and which hath foundations whose builder and maker is God.

It is by a study of these contrasts that we get a more vivid understanding of the character of the city of pure gold which is to be the final home of the redeemed from this earth. Just as there was a transition period from the age before the flood to the age after the flood, accompanied by judgment; and just as there was a transition from the Jewish age to the church age accompanied by judgment on Jerusalem and the Jews; and just as there was a transition from the church age to the kingdom age accompanied by the great tribulation judgment, so there will be a wonderful transition from the kingdom age into the age of the new creation, and this transition will be accompanied by the judgment upon the wicked dead and upon Satan.

We read that at the close of the thousand-year reign Satan must be loosed a little while out of his prison (Rev. 20:7). Many have questioned as to why Satan will be loosed again. It will be a necessity in order that he might sift out from all the nations those who had lived through the millennium in a hypocritical state of heart, and make them show their true character before the opening of the eternal ages. We are told in several places that many will serve Cod feignedly, and although no open sin will be allowed in the kingdom period, yet great multitudes during that thousand years will not yield their hearts to God and will live in a deceitful state of character, and when Satan is loosed he will work upon these hypocrites and lead them to revolt at the close of that age, and thereby manifest their inward character by rebelling preparatory to being slain. "And they went up on the breadth of the earth and compassed the camp of saints: and fire came down from God out of heaven and devoured them" (Rev. 20:9). This was all typified in the Old Testament. The reign of King Saul was a type of the law, which, as Paul said, proved to be a failure. Then the reign of David was a type of Christ in the suffering dispensation of the church age. Then the reign of King Solomon was a type of the reign of Christ in the millennium. When Solomon reigned, there was a powerful man who became his enemy, named Jeroboam, and this man fled to Egypt during the reign of Solomon – a type of the chaining of Satan during the millennium. At the end of Solomon's reign, this man, Jeroboam, returned from Egypt and led in the revolt of the ten tribes, and tried to destroy the city of Jerusalem and the tribe of Judah – an exact type that Satan, at the close of the thousand-year reign, will be let loose and lead in a great revolt against Jesus, and make a division among the people of the earth. When that revolt has been ended, by lightning coming down from the sky and killing the rebels, then the devil will be judged and cast into the lake of fire and brimstone, where the beast – the Antichrist – and the false prophet have been kept during the millennial age. Then follows the great white throne, and the wicked dead are raised and judged before the white throne.

This terminates the seven thousand years of the world's history, and closes the probationary condition of the human race. The number eight is always, in the Bible, the number for a new creation. The Jewish boy was circumcised on the eighth day – a type of the new life, the new birth, the new creation. David was the eighth son of Jesse and the founder of a new kingdom, a divine theocracy, and the one whose throne is to be perpetuated by the Lord Jesus. Christ rose on the eighth day to set forth the new creation. There were eight persons that came out of the ark after the flood to start a new world with. The new creation takes place at the beginning of the eighth thousand years of the world's history. There is never a blunder in God's Word as to dates or numbers or types or dispensations.

We have been tracing the wonderful destiny of the true front-rank saints through all the dispensations and experiences from their call out of Egypt and their regeneration on to the end; and now we have come to where we see them everlastingly fixed in immortality, and get a vision of their eternal home in the city of the living God. In our further study of this subject let us notice the following points:

1. This city is a composite structure, including both the material of the city and the inhabitants that live in it. It is called a city built of pure gold like unto clear glass, and yet it is called the Lamb's wife, and both of these descriptions are inspired and both are true. A city is a composite thing including both houses and people. If all of the inhabitants were taken out of a city and nothing left but the material buildings, it would not be a city. And, on the other hand, if all the population were scattered on a prairie or in the mountains, they of themselves would not make a city. A city must have houses, streets, material facilities, and also must have inhabitants that live and move and carry on their daily affairs of life, and both of these are equally essential to make up a city. This is just as true of the city of God as of any other city.

This New Jerusalem will be constructed of pure, transparent gold, with streets, and a river running through it, and a throne in its center, and a light beyond the brightness of the sun, with trees of life, and every possible formation of beauty and wealth and glory and convenience that the Creator can form. And it will also contain the countless millions of those who have been redeemed from the earth, including all the ranks that are mentioned in the Scriptures: prophets and apostles and evangelists and pastors and teachers and the saints; the four living creatures, and the twenty-four elders who represent multitudes of their rank from all nations, and the hundred and forty-four thousand, who are the front-rank saints gathered from Israel in their final restoration, and then the great multitude that no man can number, saved out of the great tribulation, that stand before the throne.

The city is called the bride, the Lamb's wife. That is, it is the special home and headquarters of the bridehood saints. But while the city belongs to the bride, as her special dowry and estate, as the wife of the Lamb, it will also be the home of all her companions and the virgins without number and all the redeemed of the earth. When Queen Victoria was alive she lived in Windsor Castle, which was her palace, and it was the home of all her vast family and attendants and servants, including hundreds of people; and so, in like manner, the city of pure gold is named after the Lamb's wife. But it is nonetheless the home of all who belong to that royal family, including persons of all ranks in the vast kingdom of heaven.

2. Let us notice the twelve gates in the wall of the city. "And the city had a wall great and high, and had twelve gates, and on the gates were written the names of the twelve tribes of the children of Israel. On the east three gates; on the north three gates; on the south three gates; and on the west three gates. And the twelve gates were twelve pearls; every several gate was of one pearl" (Rev. 21:12-21). This gives us a revelation of the entrance into the city. The twelve tribes of Israel set forth the covenant of the saving faith, as exhibited by Abraham, Isaac and Jacob. It is by the covenant of justification by faith that we enter into salvation, and this is the gate that admits us into the heavenly city.

The apostle, speaking of justification by faith, tells the Gentile converts that they are no longer strangers and aliens, but fellow-citizens with the saints in light. Every gate was of one pearl, so that the gates were all just alike, and this reveals to us that justification by the faith covenant is the same for all nations and kindreds and people, whether Jews or Gentiles.

The pearl, in Scripture, stands for heart purity. "Blessed are the pure in heart, for they shall see God." And the new version reads: Blessed are they that wash their robes that they may have right to the tree of life and enter through the gate into the city. Thus all these distinctive words agree, that the saints enter the New Jerusalem through the covenant of justifying faith and receive the pearl of a pure heart. Of course those can enter the city who have the gate of the city within themselves, and all those who have the pearl of heart purity will possess the very gate that admits them into the city of pure gold.

3. The Foundations in the Wall of the City: "And the wall of the city had twelve foundations, and in them the names of the twelve apostles of the Lamb. And the foundations of the wall of the city were garnished with all manner of precious stones. The first foundation was jasper; the second, sapphire; the third, a chalcedony; the fourth, an emerald; the fifth, sardonyx; the sixth, sardius; the seventh, chrysolyte; the eighth, beryl; the ninth, a topaz; the tenth, a chrysoprasus; the eleventh, a jacinth; the twelfth, an amethyst."

Just as the twelve patriarchs stand for the covenant of faith which God made to Abraham, so the twelve apostles stand for the doctrines of the Word of God concerning variety of inspired truth, and upon these doctrines the church and all saints must rest. We will not be able to understand from Scripture which doctrine was especially represented by each of the apostles, and it is not essential that we should know this matter; but we may rest assured that each of the twelve apostles in a special way represented some great cardinal doctrine and that these doctrines are the foundations referred to by the Holy Spirit when he tells us that Abraham "looked for a city which hath foundations, whose builder and maker is God." Everything in creation is founded on the Word of God, and Christ is especially the divine Word incarnate; and Paul says, "Other foundation can no man lay than that is laid, which is Christ Jesus." So when we put all the words of Scripture together concerning this subject, we gather conclusively that the foundations are the doctrines of inspired Scripture. It has been suggested, for example, that Paul in a special way stands for the doctrine of faith, and Peter for the doctrine of holiness, and John for the doctrine of love, and James for the doctrine of good works, and Jude for the doctrine of judgment, and Matthew for the kingship of Christ, and John's gospel for the deity of Christ. And thus the other apostles stand for some cardinal doctrine of which we are not informed.

There is great significance in these precious stones in connection with the foundations. The high priest in the Jewish system was to wear a breast-plate on which were the names of the twelve tribes of Israel engraved in twelve precious stones, and those twelve gems correspond to these twelve stones in the foundation of the wall of the New Jerusalem, and in fact are the same stones by name. We must also remember that the apostle Peter, in speaking of the saints, compares them to living stones, which are formed into a divine structure for the habitation of God. Both Paul and Peter speak of the saints being formed into a house for the habitation of God through the Holy Spirit.

Babylon was built of brick and was the home of backsliders, but Jerusalem was built of stone; and while the New Jerusalem is built of gold, yet the foundation walls are garnished with these twelve gems, agreeable to the character of the glorified saints, which are living stones in this divine structure. Bricks are manufactured out of clay, but these living stones grow and are not manufactured. A saint is a product of life, and each saint sets forth some type of divine life, typified by these twelve precious gems. Every one of these precious stones had a symbolic meaning, and all of them combined make up a unit of the manifold life in Christ Jesus.

We learn from this passage that the New Jerusalem is made up of saints both from the Jews and from the Gentiles; both from the twelve tribes of Israel and from the church of Christ, for while the gates are named after Israel, the foundations are named after the twelve apostles, proving that the saints of both the Old and the New Testament are combined in forming the bride of the Lamb. This proves the heresy of those who teach that the bride of Christ will be composed only of the Jews or the twelve tribes of Israel. The apostle Paul, in his epistle to the Gentile converts, makes many references to the fact that they are to be included in the number that make up the bride of the Lamb, and he says of some, that he espoused them as chaste virgins unto Christ. The bride does not include all of the body of the saved ones, but is a rib from the body, a selection of those who meet the conditions for that high rank. The apostle speaks of believers coming to Mount Zion and to the heavenly Jerusalem, to the general assembly and church of the firstborn. The general assembly includes as the original word means, the *universal gathering of all the saved ones;* but the church of the firstborn is a special selection from this universal gathering just as God told Moses that all the twelve tribes belonged to him, but that from the twelve tribes he had selected the tribe of Levi to be his firstborn. So the church of the first born corresponds exactly to those who make up the bride of Christ.

4. Notice the purity of the material of the city: "It is made of pure gold, like unto clear glass." For many years infidels disputed the reality of this inspired Scripture from the fact that gold is opaque, and how could a city made of gold be transparent? Many years ago a great chemist in England purified gold to such a degree that it became transparent like unto clear glass, and on looking through it, it gave forth a beautiful green color. Thus science proved the infallible accuracy of God's inspired Word. God knew that gold could be made transparent, thousands of years before human science demonstrated the fact. Hence the city of the New Jerusalem will be transparent, notwithstanding it is made of gold.

In all creation no metal has been found so pure and fine as gold. It has a fineness that is almost beyond human comprehension. It is said that a block of gold an inch square can be hammered out into a thin veil that will cover an acre of land, and that it can be held in suspense. Scientists have found that there is gold in the sun, from the composition of its light; and gold is in the sea, and all through the earth, and in the composition of the stars. But no element has ever been discovered so fine as gold. Thus God will make the New Jerusalem of the purest material in all his vast creation, and of such degree of purity as to be transparent like unto clear glass. It is in agreement with this fact that the saints are spoken of as being purified like unto fine gold.

The apostle speaks of having our faith like pure gold, for faith in the kingdom of heaven is just what gold is as a purchasing value on this earth. And then the bride of Christ is described in the forty-fifth Psalm as dressed in the fine gold of Ophir. So there will be a correspondence between the purity of the city and the purity of the saints who are the inhabitants.

5. Notice the size of the city. "And the city lieth foursquare, and the length is as large as the breadth, twelve thousand furlongs. The length and the breadth and the height of it are equal."

Twelve thousand furlongs in our English measure amounts to fifteen hundred miles. One corner of the city could be located in the State of Maine, and another corner in southern Florida, and the third corner in New Mexico, and the fourth corner in North Dakota; and then the structure would rise up in the sky fifteen hundred miles high. Of course these measurements are very small when compared with the magnitudes of the earth and the sun and the great solar system; but for the size of a city these measurements are beyond anything that the human mind ever dreamed of.

It is not so much the outside measurements of the city that make it so vast as it is the interior structure of the streets and-apartments and mansions and every conceivable furnishing of glory and accommodation for the glorified saints. If we allow the streets of the city to be one mile apart, and one mile high over each other, it would amount to eight million miles of streets. But if we put the streets a quarter of a mile apart and a quarter of a mile over each other, it would amount to countless millions of miles. And then if we allow the most ample space for each one of the glorified saints for a mansion, all the beings that have ever been born of the human race would only fill one corner of that structure. Thus there will be ample space for every saint to have a mansion of glory with conveniences and ornaments in some way representative of that individual's character or life work; just as the crowns that the saints wear will in some way set forth their particular rank in the kingdom, and their special rewards, so the mansion of each glorified saint will indicate in some way the peculiarities in his life or experience or work. "In my Father's house are many mansions," and this is the Father's house, and these the countless mansions in the house.

The apostle says, in verse 11, that this city has the glory of God; that is, the city is the center of divine glory and is filled with God's glory, for the Lamb is the light of it; and it has no need of the sun or the moon to shine in it, for the glory of God does lighten it, and the Lamb is the light thereof and the nations of them which are saved shall walk in the light of that city (Rev. 21:23-24).

6. We must remember also that this city is a living organism the same as our human body is. We read of the pure river of the water of life, clear as crystal, proceeding out of the throne of God and the Lamb, and that this river runs all through the city and waters the tree of life, and supplies the whole city with water. The throne of the Lamb is in the center, and some have questioned, How can this pure river flow with equal facility upwards, downwards, right or left, through every part of the city. This is explained by the fact that it will be a living organism. Look at our earth. The rivers both inside the earth and on the surface run every way, north and south and east and west and down into the earth, and also they gush up from the earth into the air. Also our human bodies are little, miniature worlds; in the center of the body is the heart, which is the source of life, sending out a river of blood with equal facility up to the head and down to the feet and out to the extremities, because it is a living organism and operates without any special reference to the law of terrestrial gravitation. The same will be true of the river of water in the New Jerusalem. It will flow every way with equal facility.

All the streets of the city will be amply supplied with beautiful trees of life, and with every variety of fruit. At least twelve manner of fruit is spoken of in this Scripture. Every curse will be removed, and every blessing that the human imagination can conceive of will be in that city. It will be in fact the crown and the consummation of all the works of God in all the created universe.

The tree of life will yield twelve manner of fruits, and yield its fruit every month, and the leaves of the tree are for healing the nations. This word "healing" more literally should be translated "health-preserving;" it does not imply that the nations will get sick, and the Greek word signifies to preserve health. So the leaves of the tree will be to preserve the perfect health of the nations throughout the ages that are to come.

"And they shall see God's face and the face of the Lamb, and his name shall be in their foreheads. And there shall be no night there; and they need no candle, neither light of the sun; and they shall reign for ever and ever. And he said unto me These are the true sayings of God" (Rev. 22).

CHAPTER 20

The Plan of the Ages

WHEN we get an insight into any of God's plans or purposes, it has the effect of drawing us to him in a stronger
affection and a more personal attachment, and also it increases
our interest in his kingdom and in his work. If a private on the
battlefield could be taken into the secret counsel of the com-
manding general and understand all the plans that the general
has for the battle, it would wonderfully increase the interest and
loyalty of the soldier, and enable him to fight with more intelligent herosim. If a clerk in a large establishment could be taken
into partnership with the firm, and have explained to him all the
details of the business and the various plans that the head men
had for carrying on the business, it would make the clerk much
more devoted to the interests of the firm and cause him to work
with more ardor and personal interest.

This same law that governs the human mind is eminently
true when applied to spiritual things and to our knowledge of
the plans of our heavenly Father, both concerning the things of
this world, and also his purpose in the mission of our lives. The
apostle tells us, in Hebrews 1:2, that God has, through his Son
Jesus, made a plan of all the ages or dispensations connected with
this world. Our English Bible reads that God, by his Son, formed
the worlds; but the word "worlds'" should be ages, and Christ was
the architect of all the various dispensations and ages of creation.

In the passage where Isaiah says that Christ should be called
the everlasting Father, it should be, "His name should he called
the Father of the Ages." There is only one God the Father, and
the word "Father" is never applied in Scripture to the Son of
God in the same way that it is applied to the first person in the

Godhead, and hence the apostle says: "To us there is but one God the Father;" that is, only one Father in the Godhead, but the Son of God is called the Father of the Ages because it was by him that all the various periods of duration were arranged. The word *eternity* occurs only once in our English Bible, but even in that passage it should be *ages,* for there is no word in the original Hebrew or Greek Scriptures that corresponds to our word eternity; the Bible teaching is that all duration has been divided off into great epochs and series of ages on ages.

God has made a special plan of the different ages belonging to our world, and the various steps of progress in the history of the human race. Each of these ages has its own peculiar features, and each successive age has various advantages over the preceding one; for all the works of God, whether in nature, grace or glory, always advance to higher degrees. Let us notice God's purposes concerning the different ages of our world, especially in reference to the probation and destiny of the human race and of his own people.

1. We may speak of the first age, extending from Adam to the flood, as the age of conscience. In that dispensation God put the human race on trial to see what man would do acting from his own conscience in connection with the work of the Spirit. God intended to prove to all the world that the human conscience, by itself, is not a sufficient guide for conduct, and this could not be proved to the satisfaction of mankind without making the experiment.

In that first dispensation there was no written law, no publication of the Ten Commandments, no church, no organized religious institution, no fixed method of religious government, no special revelation of the attributes of God, no details given as to the conduct of private life. Men claimed to be able to govern themselves and to know what was right, and so God left the race to be tried by their own consciences, to put them to the proof as to whether they would live uprightly, and worship the true God, and live in brotherly love, or whether they would develop into a race of giant sinners. Also in that age God allowed men to live a long time, practically a thousand years, in order that the living fathers might be able to transmit to their children the things concerning the creation as related by Adam, the first father; and thus these fathers, living through so many centuries, would be living books to the rising generations. Thus the people had not only truth conveyed to them concerning the things of God, but also truth emphasized by living persons and given in the spirit of fatherly affection.

Another feature of that first age was that the laws of nature were not disrupted until after the flood, and during that first dispensation there were no storms, no earthquakes, no severe winters or burning summers, but the laws of nature moved on with perfect beauty and harmony, without any sickness, without any furious demonstration from the lower animals – for the animals never ate meat and the human race never ate meat until after the flood – and so mankind had all the advantages of outward peace and prosperity. And yet, in spite of all these marvelous advantages, the nature of sin which had been caused by the fall of Adam, continually developed more and more as the centuries went on, until the wickedness of man was so great that God found it a moral necessity to destroy the race and start humanity over again from a single family.

2. The next age we may call the age of law, or the Jewish age, extending from the call of Abraham to the birth of Christ. During that dispensation God put mankind on trial again to see what would be the development of human character. During this age of law human beings not only had the conscience which they had before the flood, hut in addition to that they had a definite published law consisting of two kinds: the moral law, written in the Ten Commandments, and the ceremonial law, written by Moses, governing all the details of national and family life for the chosen family of Israelites. The moral law was written by the finger of God on tables of stones, and was for the whole race for all generations; but the ceremonial law was written by Moses and applied especially to the Hebrew people.

In this second age God also dealt with the world through one special chosen family – the children of Abraham, Isaac and Jacob. There were many advantages connected with working through one chosen family, because the family ties and affections would be a strong preservation for unity and moral strength, and also the preserving of the select seed by which the world could have the very best of instructors and rulers. That chosen family was the depositary of the revealed Word of God and the custodian of the laws of God, and they were chosen to be the teachers and leaders and missionaries for all the other nations. That chosen family also had prophets and special inspired teachers to instruct them in the things of God. The prophets of the Hebrew people, taken as a class, were the greatest men, the strongest characters, the most powerful leaders, of any class of men in the whole world, for they were infinitely superior to the poets of other nations, and also superior to the kings and generals and rulers, for they stood in with the private councils of God, and were his chosen spokesmen to the whole world, and acted in that dispensation in a similar way that the Holy Ghost was to act in a later dispensation. And yet, with all these advantages and helps in the second age, that high chosen family went astray from God, and developed forms of sin and a degree of obstinacy surpassing that of the outside Gentile nations, and their rebellion reached an awful climax in the rejection and crucifixion of the Son of God. This proved to all the universe that human character could not be thoroughly changed by mere law or by force of mental instruction, and that something else was required, to go deeper down into the character of man's soul.

3. The third dispensation we call the gospel or church age. It began with the day of Pentecost and the outpouring of the Holy Spirit, and is to extend to the second coming of Christ. In this gospel age, men still have the conscience and the moral law, and all the best things of the previous ages. In addition to this the gospel age had the personal presence and life of the Son of God incarnate in human flesh. The greatest event of its kind in the history of the universe was the incarnation of the Son of God

in a human body and soul. The fact that the second person in the infinite Godhead should come forth from the bosom of the Father and take on humanity and identify himself with a human body and soul and live a human life in this world and consent to die for the sins of the human race, is the most marvelous event in all the history of the creation of God, and we never shall be able to understand in our present life why the infinite God of the universe should select the race of mankind and this world of ours as the scene of the incarnation, and it must be that this mystery will be revealed to us in the glorified state.

The gospel age not only has the life and death of the Son of God, but also the gift of the Holy Spirit, the third person in the Trinity, to apply to man's soul the atonement of Christ and the word of Christ and to act directly on human hearts in transforming the lives of men into the image of God, and preparing them for the glorious state of existence in the ages to come.

In this age we have also the Christian church with its ministry and sacraments, and with authority to evangelize the nations and to gather out a people for the age to come. And yet in spite of these enormous advantages, the human race remains in wickedness and great darkness. There are ten times more heathen on earth today than there were when the Lord Jesus lived on this earth, and sinners multiplied a hundred times faster than believers do. The first nations that had the gospel are today the lowest and vilest of all nations on earth. Even among the nations where there are most churches and active Christians, the great mass of men are practical infidels, and manifest a hardness towards God far greater than the heathen who never have heard the gospel; and according to the words of Scripture, in this gospel age wicked men and deceivers will wax worse and worse down to the very hour when Jesus shall come again.

The first age wound up with gigantic sinners and a judgment that destroyed the people from the earth. The second age wound up with the climax of the sin of the chosen people in killing the Son of God, and was accompanied with terrible judgments in the destruction of Jerusalem and the scattering of the Jewish race. This present gospel age is winding up with great wickedness and the rankest kind of false religions, and the utter denial of the supernatural grace of God, and will be attended with the judgment of the great tribulation upon the whole world.

4. The millennial age will be the next dispensation upon our earth. This coming age will have all the advantages of the previous ages and a vast addition of blessings besides. Remember, the millennial age belongs to the probation of the world's history, and will be the period when the human race as a whole will accept the Lord Jesus Christ and countless millions will be truly regenerated and purified. In addition to the human conscience and the moral law and the gospel of the Son of God, the millennial age will have the personal presence of the glorified Jesus moving hither and thither through the air, and in all parts of the world, the same as he did in the forty days after his resurrection. The world will also have the presence and supervision of the glorified saints, who will rise in the first resurrection and, according to Scripture, have authority over the nations of the earth and superintend in every detail the affairs of the human race. Paul tells us, in Hebrews, that the angels are now sent as ministering spirits to the children of God; but he says, in the next age, that the angels will not have charge, but that the glorified saints, who have been sanctified and made one with Christ, will be made the rulers and the guardians of the world in that age, so that the education and training and management of the nations that will be born in the millennial age will be under the immediate authority and guidance of the glorified saints. In addition to these advantages, Satan will be chained and all the demons that are now acting under his authority will be chained with him in the abyss, and there will be no demon to torment or afflict any human being on the earth in that age. Also the curse will be lifted from the earth, and there will be no more briars or thorns, and the lower animals will not hurt anyone, for the lion shall eat straw like the ox; and there will be no more storms or earthquakes, for righteousness shall drop down from the clouds and truth shall spring out of the ground and nothing shall hurt or destroy. And yet, in spite of all

these marvelous blessings, we are told in several places that even in that age multitudes will serve God feignedly or deceitfully, and at the close of the millennial age, when Satan is let loose again, he will find countless thousands of hypocrites in the earth and lead them to revolt against the government of Christ, so that fire will come down out of heaven and destroy them.

Thus we see that, clear down to the end of the world's probation, man is a failure apart from the grace of God, and there is a stubbornness in sin which perpetuates itself through all the ages until it is utterly expelled by divine authority in the lake of fire with the devil and his angels.

The probation of the human race is to extend through one week, according to God's days in which it takes a thousand years to make one day. The first dispensation extended practically from Adam to the call of Abraham, two thousand years; that is, two of God's days. The second dispensation extended from the call of Abraham to the death of Christ, which was two thousand years or more, or two days. The third age extends from the death of Christ to the opening of the millennial age, which is two thousand years, or two days. This makes six days of the world's history, and all the features of God's true Sabbath will be manifested in that blessed dispensation of the seventh day.

This is God's plan for the different ages of our world's history, as related to the probation of mankind. At the close of these different ages there will start a new series of ages which is referred to so many times in the Bible by the expression "ages of ages." In every place where our English Bible reads "for ever and ever," both as applied to the duration of future punishment and to the duration of the rewards and life of the righteous, the original words are "to the ages of the ages." Hence there will be no end to the successive series of ages in the history of the universe.

This same truth applies to our individual lives, for God has a plan for each of our lives, and if we are able to understand what God's purpose is in our personal lives and our individual work that he gives us to do, it becomes a marvelous inspiration to our hearts to be perfectly devoted to him and his work in the kingdom.

CHAPTER 21

The Three Appearings of Christ

WHENEVER Christ has made a manifestation of himself as the Son of God throughout the history of creation, it has always constituted an epoch, and been the occasion of great events and the setting forward of some new dispensation of divine providence or grace. He first appeared out from the bosom of the Father in the act of creation: for by him all things were created, and without him nothing was made, that was made. Thus his first appearance from the Father formed the epoch of the creation of the universe. When he appeared to Adam in the garden of Eden, it formed the epoch of the starting of human history, and the setting up of Adam and Eve as the rulers of this lower world. When he appeared to Noah it was to reveal to him the coming of the flood, and to give instructions concerning the building of the ark for the saving of his family. When he appeared to Abraham it was the epoch of calling out one chosen family from whom should come a chosen race that should be God's agents in revealing divine truth to mankind, and out of which race should come the incarnate Son of God. When he appeared to Moses at the burning bush, it was another epoch, of delivering Israel from bondage, and giving the law, and instituting the kingdom of Israel. When he appeared to David, it was to make a covenant with him concerning the kingdom of God, involving the promise that the seed of David should reign upon his throne forever. When he appeared as a babe in Bethlehem in human flesh, it was the fulfillment of a great many prophecies and the first step in instituting the world's redemption and the kingdom of heaven. There are three other special appearings of Christ which are mentioned in the 9th chapter of Hebrews, each of which forms a special epoch in the history of redemption. It is a very remarkable portion of Scripture.

"For Christ is not entered in the holy places made with hands, which are the figures of the true; but into heaven itself, now to *appear* in the presence of God for us; not as the high priest entereth often into the holy places made with hands with the blood of others; for then must he often have suffered since the foundation of the world: but now once in the end of the world (or, more properly, at the consummation of the age) hath he *appeared* to put away sin by the sacrifice of himself. So Christ was once offered to bear the sins of many; and unto them that look for him shall he *appear* the second time without sin (or without a sin offering) unto salvation" (Heb. 9:24-28).

Let us take time to study carefully the three appearings that are referred to in this portion of the Word. He appeared to put away sin; and then he appeared in the presence of God up in heaven for us; and in due time he will return and appear the second time to those who look for him.

1. He appeared to put away sin. The literal rendering of the words is: At the consummation of the ages he appeared to put away sin. We all know that the world has not come to an end, and so it is incorrect to say that he appeared at the end of the world to put away sin; and the revised version has corrected the translation. The word "age" or "ages" refers to a dispensation, for the entire history of the world is marked off by different ages or dispensations. The first age was from Adam to Noah's flood. In that age they had no law, no Bible, no church, but the human race was put on trial to be governed by the human conscience, which was operated on by the Holy Spirit, for God said to Noah: "My Spirit shall not always strive with men." The power of conscience was not equal to guide the race either in morals or salvation, and that age came to a close. With Moses came the institution of another age or dispensation – that of the law, which included the moral law in the Ten Commandments, and the ceremonial law, and also the ministry of prophets, and types. The law could not save anyone, but its office was to reveal sin, and show the need of

salvation. The law age having fulfilled its purpose in revealing sin, came to a close, and then Jesus appeared, the incarnate Son of God, to make a sacrifice for the sins of the world, and to provide the salvation which the law had proved to be a necessity. Hence Christ did not appear as a Savior at the end of the conscience age, but at the end of the law age, because it was the law which revealed sin, and also revealed the penalty for sin, and so showed the necessity of a sacrifice sufficient to make an atonement for the sins of men.

The word "appear" is very significant when we take it in the light of the crucifixion of Christ. The crucifixion of Jesus was one of the most conspicuous things that has ever happened in the world's history. As the apostle says, it was not done in a corner. The spot where Christ was crucified was outside the city of Jerusalem to the north, on a high hill a hundred feet above the city, and from that standpoint nearly the whole of Palestine can be seen. Men could have stood down by the Dead Sea, over twenty miles southeast of Jerusalem, and with a good spy-glass could have seen Christ hanging on the cross. Men could have stood on Mount Hebron, about twenty miles south of Jerusalem, where Abraham, Isaac and Jacob are all buried, and with a good spy-glass could have seen Christ die on Mount Calvary. From several places along the shores of the Mediterranean, men with good spyglasses could have seen the crucifixion. From Mount Carmel, where Elijah prayed fire from heaven, men could stand and with good spyglasses could have seen Christ on the cross. And then from away up north, on Mount Lebanon, with a telescope men could have seen Christ hanging on the cross. Every human being on earth at that time could have been so located in Palestine, that with good spyglasses, they could have seen Christ on the cross. It is simply marvelous to see how God arranged to have his dear Son die in such a locality as to have made it possible for all the human race to see him die; and this gives wonderful force to the words of the apostle, he appeared, to put away sin."

But this significant truth has another application, and that is, in order that Christ may be a Savior he must appear by faith to each individual penitent, for it is by looking to Christ crucified that we receive remission of sins. Countless instances can be related of penitents having visions of Christ at the time their sins are forgiven. The late Col. Henry Hadley told me many years ago, that when he bowed at the altar in old Water Street Mission in New York to seek Jesus, that during that day he had taken sixty drinks of liquor, and fell down at the old mourners' bench, two hundred and twenty five pounds of lager beer and sin; and he said that while he was there weeping, in a drunken state, he had a vision of the crucifixion of Jesus, and became unconscious to everything around him, and he saw them take Christ and nail him to the cross, and heard the blows of the hammer on the nails, and saw the blood spurt out from his hands and feet; and that from the moment he had that vision, all his sins were taken away and all desire for liquor was utterly removed from his system.

Some years ago an actress on the stage of a theater was suddenly arrested by seeing a vision of the crucified Savior in one of the galleries, and screamed out that she would give herself to Jesus; and from that moment was thoroughly changed in her heart and life.

When I was seeking the Lord to forgive my sins, as a soldier boy in the Southern army, on the 12th day of August, 1863, I became unconscious of everything around me, and had a vision of Jesus with his hands stretched out; and from that moment my burden was gone and I was supremely happy. Instances like this may occur to only a few people, comparatively, but in some way Christ must appear to the faith of the true seekers, in order that their sins may be taken away. The word for faith, in the Old Testament, is *to look.* "They looked unto him and were lightened." "Look unto me, all ye ends of the earth." Hence both in a historical sense and in an individual sense, there must be an appearance of Christ as a sin-bearer, a sacrifice, an atonement, to take away our sins. And then what significance there is in the words, "to put away sin." Not to repress sin or to cover it over, but to actually remove it, put it away, put it out of our sight; and God says he also puts it out of his own sight. Christ is the only one in all the universe that can remove sin from the sinner, and separate the soul from its guilt and shame.

The appearance of Christ to Paul on his way to Damascus is familiar to every Bible reader.

2. "He appears in the presence of God for us in heaven." After finishing his work on the earth, and having spent forty days in a resurrected and glorified body to complete the testimony of his resurrection power and authority, he ascended in the presence of witnesses up into heaven, to the right hand of God the Father, where he has been all the centuries since, appearing before God for us.

This was all set forth in the ceremonial priesthood, where, on the great day of atonement the high priest sacrificed the animals in the presence of the people and the other priests, and then took the blood in a basin and disappeared from the people and the other priests, and went beyond the second veil where they could not see him, and appeared before God under the wings of the cherubim, and sprinkled the blood on the mercy seat to make an atonement for the people, and to intercede for the people, and to finish the work that was assigned to him in the divine presence. Thus Christ fulfilled every point in that ceremonial: for he shed his own blood in the presence of countless thousands who had assembled at Jerusalem for the great Passover, and when he was hurried he disappeared from the eyes of the world, and three days after, when he arose, he took his own blood up into heaven and sprinkled it on the mercy seat before God the Father according to the exact prescription of the law, and returned that same day, and spent forty days living in the air and appearing at various times to chosen witnesses.

Jesus never commenced his work as a high priest until after his resurrection. The apostle Paul tells us explicitly that if Christ were on the earth he would not be a priest, because the Levitical priests performed all the services belonging on the earth; but Paul affirms that Christ became a priest, doing the work of a priest, after his resurrection; for he was made a priest after the order or rank of Melchizedek, and not according to the rank of Aaron.

Very few Christians have ever put together the things that Christ performs while he appears in heaven in the presence of God. There are several items mentioned in Scripture which describe the occupation of Jesus while he appears in heaven. I have already mentioned one of those significant acts, and that is, the sprinkling of his own blood upon the mercy-seat in the presence of God the Father. It is a great mistake to think that the blood of Christ remained lying on the ground, because it is the teaching of Scripture that the blood of atonement must be taken and sprinkled on the mercy-seat in the holy of holies. According to the words of Saint Paul, "Christ is a high priest of good things to come, by a greater and more perfect tabernacle, not made with hands, neither by the blood of goats and calves, but by his own blood he entered in once into the holy place, having obtained eternal redemption for us" (Heb. 9:11-12).

From the time that the high priest shed the blood of the animal on the great day of atonement, no one must touch him until after he had sprinkled the blood on the mercy-seat in the second veil and returned out from that veil, and then they could touch him. This explains the passage in John's Gospel, where, when Mary first saw the risen Lord she attempted to take hold of his garment, but he said to her, "Touch me not, for I have not yet ascended to my Father, but go tell my disciples that I ascend." And the word "ascend" is in the present tense, which means just now, at this moment, I ascend to my Father and your Father, to my God and your God. An hour after this, Christ appeared again, to the disciples, and they caught him by the knees and worshiped him, proving that in the interval between the time when Mary first saw him, and the time when he appeared to the disciples, he had ascended and taken his own blood and sprinkled it on the mercy-seat before God the Father and had returned back to the earth.

Another thing that Christ performs while he appears in the presence of the Father is the outpouring of the Holy Spirit upon believers. It is true that Christ gave a measure of the Spirit to the disciples before his permanent ascension, but that was the Holy

Spirit in the form of a breath, which accompanies the gift of life, and which was the assurance or witness of the Spirit to their hearts that they were the children of God; but after his permanent ascension to the Father he then poured out the Holy Spirit as the divine Comforter, the promised baptism of the Spirit, the sanctifier, that the Holy Spirit should possess the church, and take the place of Christ on earth, and remain with the church to the end of the age, when Christ will return. Hence the Lord Jesus, in the presence of God, has authority to bestow the Holy Spirit, not only to the church but to individuals, and also by the Holy Spirit to impart various gifts to believers. Christ had no authority to give the Holy Ghost to anybody in the world during his lifetime, until after his resurrection, and then he testified, saying, "All authority is given unto me in heaven and in earth." It was by his death and resurrection that he acquired authority from the Father to administer the Holy Spirit, and all spiritual gifts, as well as to administer through the Spirit all matters of divine providence.

Another work that Christ is performing in the presence of God is that of intercession. Several times this work of his intercession with the Father is mentioned in Scripture. Some have inquired if Jesus, up in heaven, prays for sinners. The saying is that Christ prayed while hanging on the cross, "Father, forgive them, for they know not what they do," and Christ has certainly not backslidden, for he is the same yesterday, today, and forever; and if he prayed for sinners while dying on the cross, he certainly prays for them at the present time in the presence of the Father, and pleads for them the merit of his blood that lies on the mercy-seat. And most certainly he prays for all believers, and he still perpetuates that wonderful prayer he offered, in the 17th chapter of John's Gospel, in which he prays to the Father to sanctify the disciples through his own truth; and we may be sure that that prayer is still offered to the Father.

Another work that Christ is performing up in heaven is that of preparing the many mansions for the glorified saints to have as their homes. "In my Father's house are many mansions. I go to prepare a place for you; and if I go to prepare a place for you, I will come again and receive you to myself." The construction of the city of pure gold is the most marvelous thing in all the material universe of God. He was six days creating the heavens and the earth; but he has been nearly two thousand years building and furnishing the many mansions.

These are some of the things which are made known in Scripture that Christ is carrying forward while he is absent from this earth, and while he is appearing in the presence of the Father.

3. He will appear again the second time back to this earth. When we read, "He will appear the second time without sin unto salvation," we must remember that the word "sin" here refers to a sin offering. When Christ first appeared he was a sin offering on the cross, to put away sin; but at his second appearing back to the earth he will not be a sin offering, but the Judge and King of all the world – to judge mankind as to how they have treated the sin offering which he made, as to what relation they sustain towards himself.

There is a beautiful parallel between the 9th chapter of Hebrews and the 9th chapter of Leviticus. In the 9th of Leviticus there is a description of the sacrifices that the high priest was to offer on the great day of atonement: After the high priest had finished his work in shedding the blood and sprinkling it upon the altar, he was then to come out from the second veil, and lift up his hands towards the people and bless them, and then come down from offering the sin offering, and come out and bless the people; and when he did that, the glory of the Lord appeared to all the people, and fire came out from before the Lord and consumed upon the altar the burnt offering; and when all the people saw this they shouted and fell on their faces. How perfectly this sets forth the priestly ministry of the Lord Jesus, that he is to come out from the tabernacle on high, and lift up his hands and bless his saints, and appear to his people in glory accompanied bv divine fire, and his saints will fall on their faces and give God the glory, preparatory to being translated and caught up to meet the Lord in the air. It is beautiful to notice in how many instances there are parallel chapters in the Bible, and this is one of those instances.

It is also worth our while to notice the words, "Unto them that look for him shall he appear the second time." There is something in believers' looking for the second coming of the Lord which puts upon them a character of faith and watchfulness, and is often referred to in Scripture as to a New Testament believer, as in that passage where Paul speaks of certain believers coming behind no other church in all gifts, waiting for the coming of the Lord, as if that attitude of waiting and looking for Christ was one of the genuine marks of Christian discipleship.

Another word in this connection is "salvation." "He will appear the second time unto salvation." The word "salvation" is used in several ways in the New Testament, as, for instance, it sets forth a temporal salvation and a spiritual salvation, as where the apostle says that Christ is the Savior of all men, but especially of them that believe. That is, Christ is the Savior of all men in a temporal sense in preserving them alive, in giving them opportunity of hearing the gospel. But he is in a special way the Savior from sin to those who believe. And then the Scriptures teach an initial salvation and a perfect salvation, for it speaks of believers whose sins are pardoned, and yet urges them to go on to perfection, to a full salvation. And then the Scriptures speak of a present salvation and an eternal salvation, for with regard to salvation from sin, this is the day of salvation. And yet the word is many times used in reference to eternal salvation, as where Peter says, "There is a grace to be brought unto you at the revelation of Jesus Christ" (1 Peter 1:13). And also in Heb. 1:14, that the angels are ministering spirits to those who shall be the heirs of salvation – or more literally, to those believers who are just about to become heirs of eternal salvation. Hence the word "salvation" in the passage under consideration refers to the salvation in the glorified state, not only from all sin and guilt, but from all mortality, sickness, pain, infirmity, and every circumstance connected with our present condition of trial in this life.

Christ must appear the second time in order to reap the harvest of His first appearing.

A farmer makes two visits to a wheat field. At the first visit he appears in the field to plow the soil and sow the seed, and put everything in good condition for a crop. After four months he makes a second appearance on the field to reap the harvest and garner his grain. And this sets forth that Christ, at his first coming, sowed the seed of his Word, and shed his blood, and poured out the Spirit, that he might have a harvest of souls from the earth. In due time he will appear the second time, back to the same field where he preached and bled, in order to reap the golden grain – the souls that have been regenerated and purified by his grace.

He must also appear the second time in order to set up his kingdom. The first word that God ever spoke about making man was that he must have dominion and reign as a king, so that the kingdom idea is the first that God ever expressed with regard to the human race and this earth. The first word that Jesus ever preached was with regard to the kingdom of heaven, a kingdom composed of a second-born race, and of resurrected and glorified men, a kingdom that should be like the King himself, that should come down from heaven and occupy this earth. The church age is but preparatory to the kingdom age. The church is not the kingdom, but a company of believers gathered out from all nations, kindreds and tongues and qualified to be the officers and the priests who are to exercise their functions of rulership in the kingdom. The church age is for the saving and perfecting of believers to amply qualify them for the glorious functions of being kings and priests in the ages that are to come. One more fact in connection with the second coming of Christ is that his appearance will have a divine power to instantly transform and glorify the believers who have received him in the church age; for the apostle John says, "When he shall appear, we shall be like him, for we shall see him as he is."

THE END

Buy online at our website: **www.KingsleyPress.com**
Also available as an eBook for Kindle, Nook and iBooks.